MW01015691

Dear En... May your fr... never cease ... over this be... planet. May ... wandering ... to a ... of ... the hea... your ... with gratitude, (ap...) xx

BACKPACKER'S

PRACTICAL AND SPIRITUAL GUIDE TO THE UNIVERSE

BookVenture Publishing LLC
1000 Country Lane Ste 300
Ishpeming MI 49849
www.bookventure.com
Hotline: 1(877) 276-9751
Fax: 1(877) 864-1686

Ordering Information:
Quantity sales. Special discounts are available on quantity purchases by corporations, associations, and others. For details, contact the publisher at the address above.

Printed in the United States of America

Library of Congress Control Number:		2015948912
ISBN-13:	Softcover	978-1-943265-71-8
	Pdf	978-1-943265-72-5
	ePub	978-1-943265-73-2
	Kindle	978-1-943265-74-9

Rev. date: 09/30/2016

Disclaimer
This publication is designed to provide accurate and personal experience information in regard to the subject matter covered. It is sold with the understanding that the author, contributors, publisher are not engaged in rendering counselling or other professional services. If counseling advice or other expert assistance is required, the services of a competent professional person should be sought out.

BACKPACKER'S

PRACTICAL AND SPIRITUAL GUIDE TO THE UNIVERSE

Gaylyn Morgan

DEDICATED TO MY adventurous and eternally optimistic parents – Col and Shirl.

Special thanks to my darling husband and captain, Thomas for asking me to share his incredible adventure of sailing around the world and encouraging me every step of the way with writing this book.

And with lots of love to Samantha and Kenett.

A big thanks to my editor and friend, Junxiu Lu.

A big thanks to all my blog followers and dear friends who encouraged me in writing a book.

Introduction

MY NAME IS Gaylyn and I have lived both an ordinary and extraordinary life. I am far from your movie perfect person with a movie perfect life but I am happy, fulfilled and live life with purpose. I have been putting this book together for the last few years. It was inspired by my own journeys, the experiences that have made me who I am, and all the people I have met along the way. I align with no official religion but have adopted my own belief system from my own experiences and this has influenced my attitude to life and is reflected in this book.

This book is written out of a love for travel and is something to grab and read on all occasions: preparing for a trip; getting excited for a trip; picking yourself up off the ground after life knocks you down; to remind yourself how great you are. It is a simple but delicious recipe for inspiration.

Travelling with the Universe is about altering intermittently between being in control and letting go. You'll learn to know the difference and when each is required. Enjoy the book and enjoy the journey.

Freedom

It is not afraid,
It is fearless.
It is not selfish,
It is generous.
It is not judgemental,
It is open-minded.
It is not irresponsible,
It is thoughtful.
It is not cost free,
It is priceless.
It is not homeless,
It is belonging.
It is not reckless,
It is mindful.
It is not lonely,
It is loving.

Why?

Travel is fatal to prejudice, bigotry, and narrow-mindedness, and many of our people need it sorely on these accounts. Broad, wholesome, charitable views of men and things cannot be acquired by vegetating in one little corner of the earth all one's lifetime.

— Mark Twain, The Innocents Abroad/Roughing It

THE UNIVERSE IS a spectacular place full of intricacies and delights. We need not limit ourselves to earthly pleasures but have a sense of exploring beyond the obvious. Just because we physically can't leave the planet (well, on a backpacker's budget anyway), it doesn't mean we can't explore the universal laws that govern the galaxies and pick up on "the vibe". Thinking in this way creates a mindset that opens a type of endless beauty. We are a part of this beauty. Observing the Universe's unique way of renewing, nurturing and keeping balance will enhance your interactions with each other and with your world as you travel.

Travelling helps us to cherish the main purposes in life and to make the most of opportunities that come our way. Numerous conversations and reflections throughout my lifetime have taught me that we are here for three main purposes:

1. Relationships — How we break the cycles of bad behaviour within them and move all of humanity towards a more open-minded, harmonious and just community. Throughout life we are learning how to make our relationships fulfilling and how to bring joy to those around us. You are responsible for all of your relationships. You can never blame someone else for them and you are not responsible for any other two people's

relationship either. If some members in your family or wolf pack don't get along as well as you'd like them to, well it's just none of your business. It's their journey and you don't have to be concerned for them. Trust them to work out what is best. Sure, when asked give advice or guide someone, but don't take on the emotions of other people's relationships. You've got enough to deal with.

2. Experiences—We are filled with information about life and destinations but we need to live it to truly understand it. That means that you're not just a passenger – you're at the helm driving life in the direction that you want it to go. We are here on this earth to learn to understand about our world and the people within it. There is a difference between knowing something and understanding it. When we live a life by 'doing' we are moving from 'knowing' something to 'understanding' it. We pass on our understandings to others through shared interactions that also help them to live a more fulfilling life.

3. Making a difference—In some form we are here to make the world a better place than when we arrived. We all have an influence on other people's lives and we should always be conscious to be a 'good' difference. It is often through our work that we can truly make a difference. Finding our true purpose in life is difficult for most people because we get caught up with materialistic ambitions and forget to listen to our inner voice. Somewhere along our journey we get to identify this purpose and it gives us an inner drive. Finding what brings you joy is one way to pinpoint this purpose. Learn to pick up on what resonates with you and take action that drives your life in that direction. We should all be doing something that brings us joy. Everyone in the world should be happy in their work and finding happiness in it. Paid or unpaid, it is all about an energy exchange. What are you giving and what are you receiving in return? Often once one purpose is

fulfilled another purpose arrives. They're often interrelated and meaningful at different parts of our lives.

As we travel, a kaleidoscope of options for our future is put on display as our skills develop. We learn to adapt and cope with unforeseen circumstances, equipping us with a toolbox of vital skills that are sought after in the business and private worlds.

Our minds open as we witness varied approaches and attitudes towards love, work and living. By understanding how others live and enjoy life, we develop an appreciation for differences and realise that 'our' way isn't the only way. We go beyond tolerance of differences and recognise they are an asset in creating success in this diverse world. There is something to learn from every place you visit and every person you meet. Travel allows you to find all the different versions of people and places that will shape your mind for the better.

We learn to be respectful. When we are travelling to new countries we are, first and foremost, guests of that country. As guests there are expectations about our behaviour and the amount of respect we need to give to our hosts. Of course there will be an impact due to the cultural exchange but our aim should always be to make it a positive one. We learn to show care for others and our own culture.

Travelling teaches us some of the most important lessons in life. As far as every soul is concerned, one of the major things we need to learn is to 'step lightly' during our time here on earth. By this I mean we need to leave only joy and happiness without making a gaping hole in the world's resources or causing damage. As we move throughout the different continents we learn to consider other people's needs through new and wonderful experiences. We learn to travel lightly and to rely on a minimum amount of material items that we require so we learn to appreciate a more sustainable lifestyle. We realise that we don't need a lot of 'things' in this Universe to be truly happy. When observing people living uncomplicated lives, yet displaying such overwhelming generosity, helps us to make the different realisations. On many occasions we know it but are yet to understand it. Always ask yourself in a new place, 'What brings joy to the people who live here?'

Being happy and joyful along the way helps us all to step lightly on this earth. Our physical needs are lessened. We save on the earth's resources and the future inhabitants will thank us for that. We can come to the conclusion that material items are limited as tools for happiness. And this leaves more money for more travel.

Wandering about in a forest or on a beach gives you time to think. You'll have time to think about your life – what you want out of it and what you want to accomplish. Creativity feeds off this space that you're giving yourself and you are offering yourself the opportunity to manifest ideas. You will learn how to make this space, even once you are caught up in life.

The old cliché that it's "all about the journey" is true to a point but life is also about the beautiful moments that find their way into your heart and remain imprinted on your soul throughout your life. They are the moments that capture your imagination and define who you are. They are the moments that give you the insight of what brings you joy. And let's face it, this life should be about joy; giving it, feeling it and always aiming for it in all that we do. Finding the joy in the moment teaches us to live for the now without having complicated expectations for the future. The tools that we need to take into the future are anticipation, hope and love without worrying about the details.

How we best achieve these universal goals is dependent on our skills, desires and the people we have surrounded ourselves with. But like my dad always said, "Life owes you nothing kid. You have to get out and grab it." This book is about being an active participant in your own life and to also know when to let go of the steering wheel. It is your journey. Make it happen the way you want it to. You're in the driver's seat.

So many books have been written about the beautiful places you can visit. There are lots of guides to read about different destinations that will help you to plan your journey in finer detail. The world is filled with magic and an array of people to meet and learn about. It boils down to individual choice about where you choose to actually travel. Everyone's priorities will be different and this will lead many to different corners of the world. Some places will be well-worn tourist spots while others will be out-of-the-way adventure destinations. Either kind of place leads you towards finding out new things about yourself.

But no matter where you go, you will always have YOU. You can't run away from this. If there's something about you that you want to change, this is the time to do it.

THIS MUCH CHANGE IS NEVER A BURDEN!

How to use this Guidebook

This handbook is about making the most out of your travel, staying safe, and reaching the potential that you are capable of obtaining. Inside are also many tips about preparing for your journey. It's about learning to love and appreciate the person you are (if you don't already) and loving the world you're in. It's about dispelling destructive thought patterns and creating your own positive future. Ultimately, you will use the book however you want to. I am hoping that you find it flexible and light enough to carry with you so that you'll be able to refer back to it along the way. Some sections may not resonate with you; this will be because you may not be ready to hear those messages or you may be beyond them. Other sections you will continuously return to so that the message within really sinks in. May I suggest that you colour code some of them so that you can revisit an item that may reassure you or remind you of a lesson needed. There is space at the end of each chapter for you to jot down notes and add to the messages I have written. Hopefully you will be relating all the information to yourself. Sometimes I repeat a topic that I'm using to illustrate a point. This is to cater for those readers who like to flick through a book, only reading bits and pieces that interest them.

As far as the recipes go — don't wait to be on the road to try them. This is a budget way of surviving in your own home as well. They are environmentally friendly because it reduces wastage and requires minimum energy to cook. Send me your own quick recipes and ideas about saving money with food so I can pass them on to others. This book is about creating a network of travellers and like-minded people as well. You can contact me or contribute through my website listed in the appendix.

Many of the travelling tips can be utilised on smaller trips or in your own home. It's really about opening up your mind to make the most out of your life journey, remaining positive, optimistic and loving what you're doing in each moment.

The second part of the book includes short stories from my travels from all through the years, in no particular order. They are purely for illustration of points made throughout the book and for entertainment. I'm sure you'll have lots of your own to add to it.

In the back of the book I have added a bit of space for you to write notes or to include your own stories. These can only be positive and helpful or the book may self-combust.

There's a section on helpful websites including a link to my own blog and my website. I haven't gone overboard with these because websites change so often so I've also listed some possible 'searches' that may help lead you to more information. As a result anything could appear and your discretion, as with all things, is required.

I will be available for card readings if you would like a more personalised approach as long as I have access to the internet or we're in the same location. I'm always keen to meet new people. All emails to me will get a response but it just may take time if I'm out on the ocean or in the wilderness.

Most of all I hope that your journey is full of wonderful learning opportunities that help you to learn to deal with whatever life throws at you and lasting memories and friendships that will bring you a lot of joy in the future.

Happy Travelling.

Content

Part 1

Vibe

Brazil is not what you see but what you feel. Once you spend time here –
a week, two weeks – you get in the vibe. It's really intoxicating.

—Francisco Costa

In New York it seems like there's no Monday or Saturday or Sunday. The
town is always moving. The vibe is great.

—Thierry Henry

NOT ONE OF us can deny that, at any time, we can walk into a room and within a matter of moments do an automatic diagnosis of the vibe there. It's a human trait, an ability, that assists us with our survival instincts. We are all vibrating at a particular frequency and if we are 'in tune' with a certain location, we resonate with it. We will make the most of our time there and accomplish what it is we are meant to be gaining from that place.

Recognising the significance of this vibration assists us in intuitively knowing where we are meant to be and who we are meant to be with. If the vibe isn't right, we should leave. If the vibe feels good, then we're moving our lives in a forward motion. Consciously being aware of this vibration is our ticket to being in the right place at the right time, avoiding a disaster, meeting the person of your dreams and being attracted to the right group of people. Discarding or ignoring this vibe and attraction could ultimately land you in deep water or have you miss out on an amazing opportunity.

The most incredible aspect of this vibe is that you can not only be aware of it, but you can change it through choice. It is the power of your thoughts that can do this. Joseph Sproats, the highly acclaimed Australian author, lecturer and psychologist, describes this as Vibrational Psychology and states that "by purposefully recognising those moments when a vibe alters, we are able to make an appropriate action". He also explains that this conscious behaviour drives us to the point of attraction and it is in this moment that we directly lead ourselves to self-fulfillment and a sense of achievement.

It is the point of decision making that will have the most impact on our lives and we can drive those alterations in the vibe through our feelings, opinions and our choice of language. How we choose to react and interact will determine how closely we are moving towards what we are trying to achieve. By staying positive and enthusiastic we can generate a positive experience for those around us. It's like sailing with the Trade Winds. When you go west at the right time of the year, you trim your sails occasionally to get the most out of your boat; the wind drives you forward seemingly effortlessly. But if you don't leave port at the right time, you are in for a hard sail; beating against the waves and wind, taking longer to reach your destination, arriving exhausted. You are making life difficult for yourself. By being thoughtful in our responses and staying focused with what it is that we want out of life, we can create the results we are looking for.

But If you've had a tough run in life or day so far, or you think you have, you can turn this around with the power of thought so your journey goes more smoothly. We need to be able to understand the good because of the bad; it's polarity – yin and yang, karma, Newton's third law. Take the aspects of your life where you have had challenging relationships, situations, and what appears to be bad luck, but instead focus on any facets where learning has occurred. Reflect on how you became a better person because of those trials and tragedies in your life. You can't change what has happened but you can certainly focus on the future and how the skills you've developed through the turmoil can benefit you now.

Tip Box

Feel your own energy – your vibe. Rub your hands together quickly and then slowly pull your palms apart and then together again making out you're playing an accordion. You will feel your own energy and maybe even sparks. It's a spongy, warm feeling. Your energy is a vital component to any destination's energy. You become a part of the place. Feeling positive and enthusiastic with anticipation heightens the experience of any location and interaction. You have the power to influence others around you in a positive or negative way also. Try to always make it a positive impact. You have the control to ensure you have a great time on your journey. Use that power wisely to move your life forward.

There are many stories of survival where the power of positive thinking has kept a person alive. Any survival manual will state 'knowing that you will survive' contributes the most to a successful outcome. Having the skills to survive under extreme conditions comes in handy, but the will to survive and the sheer acceptance that will be the result is the most contributing factor to staying alive. Not only do these people live, but they get to write a book and sign up for a movie contract afterwards. Just look at the subject of '127 Hours,' Aron Ralston who cut his own arm off to survive and Erik Weihenmayer, the first sight impaired person to climb Mt. Everest. Their ability to control their own environment and destiny is truly inspirational.

Fear works in the same way. By focusing on what you fear the most attracts that event into your life. We all get a bit worried about things in our lives at some time, we're human. So when we find that we are over-analysing or focusing too hard on a negative aspect, we have to take charge of our thoughts and steer our life back in the direction that we want. We do this by activating positive thoughts and avoiding focus on the negative. Not only that, we put a plan into action and we change our behaviours as a result of our thoughts.

A friend of mine told me a story that illustrates this point. Every time her husband walked through the tropical oasis that they'd built and grown, he would see a few flying foxes hanging in a tree. He would see them and worry that a colony of these mammals would possibly move into his forest and take over, killing the trees. My friend advised him to take a different path through the garden so that he wouldn't see them and therefore wouldn't be reminded of his fear. This action averted his thoughts towards more positive things. The flying foxes have stayed away. Sometimes we need to take a different path. You need to ask yourself if your behaviour is really focusing on the ultimate outcome of your situation and check that your thoughts and your actions are in tune with the desired result.

Tip Box

Examples of how to change your behaviours to lead your life in the direction that you want.

- Wanting to have enough money for your journey – put a budget into place and stick to it.
- Wanting that special career – develop the skills needed to go for it.
- Wanting to be popular and have plenty of friends – act kindly, be trustworthy and avoid nasty gossip – be a fun seeker, (and wash regularly).
- Worried about putting on too much weight – take care of what you drink, eat less, eat healthy and exercise.
- Wanting to attract that special someone – be the person who you would want to have in your life.
- Want to travel – get a passport and book a ticket to somewhere.
- **Whinging** is not a strategy for success. If you have a complaint about your life – do something about it.
- **Be proactive.**

Understanding these concepts of recognising and altering the vibe places you in a unique position to direct your life on any path you want. You are responsible for your own life. You learn to flow with the Universe rather than fight against it. You are able to trust more freely because you know that you are in a position of control of your own life. There will always be challenges, but life would be boring without them. They are unavoidable and they force us to grow. It is how you deal with them that is important; and travelling gives you a wealth of opportunities to learn, to test the vibe and to shape your future.

Notes

Trust

No one else will make your life happen for you. You have to trust yourself to get things done. The rest, the Universe will take care of.

—Gaylyn

I have come to accept the feeling of not knowing where I am going. And I have trained myself to love it. Because it is only when we are suspended in mid-air with no landing in sight, that we force our wings to unravel and alas begin our flight. And as we fly, we still may not know where we are going to. But the miracle is in the unfolding of the wings. You may not know where you're going, but you know that so long as you spread your wings, the winds will carry you.

—C. Joybell

TRUST IS THE beginning of success in any relationship but especially the relationship that you have with yourself. So the first thing to do is to critically examine if you really are cut out for travelling with the Universe. That means handing a whole lot of trust over to situations that don't appear to be in your control anymore. We get very comfortable in our own zone where there is a high amount of predictability. In our daily lives we count on that predictability and usually manipulate our surroundings so we avoid major change. Change can cause stress because we're having to rethink our strategies of engagement with our surroundings and with others. Can you really live without those creature comforts of knowing basically when and what is occurring? Can you trust yourself to take life as it comes and relax when things don't appear to be going as planned? Deciding to go travelling is a huge leap of faith in yourself. Make sure it's something that you really want to do and not just someone else's suggestion.

As a traveller, you'll learn to adapt quickly to unforeseen circumstances and your attitude towards these situations will be the catalyst for development. In order to make the most of the changes that will occur on your journey, it will pay to adopt a suitable attitude before you even leave. Devising plans A and B mentally prepares you for alternatives. Sometimes having a backup plan can help you to remain calm. There are many good relaxation techniques that can help you to adopt a tranquil persona. These can ensure you have the space for making good decisions. Rushing decisions can be the major cause of lost belongings, accidents or finding yourself in a bad situation. So always give yourself plenty of time to focus on the vibe when you're on the move. By giving yourself that space to think things through, you will develop strategies for dealing with cancelled planes, lost phones, missing documents, etc. These skills will build resilience and can be transferrable to other areas of your life. You may even get to the point where you realise you can take your hands off the steering wheel and enjoy an unplanned journey.

Tip Box

Out of Body Relaxation Technique

- Sit or lie down and concentrate on your breathing. Take in slow long breaths through your nose and let it slowly out through your mouth.
- Close your eyes.
- Continue for five or so breaths.
- Concentrate on feeling the vibration of every cell in your body. Begin at the toes and work your way up to your scalp.
- Then imagine your body resonating and floating just above your body.
- Feel it floating there.
- Maintain this position for 5 or 10 minutes.
- You will feel like you have slept for hours.

Deliberately leaving things to chance opens up a whole new sense of 'being'. Once you find yourself 'going with the flow' you will recognise a cognitive shift in who you are. This doesn't mean that you're inactive. You are still being proactive about discovery because you're choosing to be less driven by internal desires but instead, handing over a certain amount of control. You're beginning not to fear change. You've learned to understand that change can also be exciting and stimulating, opening a whole world of adventure and growth. Weather conditions or local politics can force you to deviate from a well-planned excursion and take you off onto an entirely unexpected path. No matter where it takes you, there will be opportunities to learn and see new wonders. You just have to trust that it was 'meant to be' so you could acquire new understandings and experiences. This is a shift in your level of trust with the Universe.

Living in fear of change usually keeps people safely locked up in their comfort zone, finding excuses not to deviate away from the 'norm'. Nearly all of your friends will tell you to stay safe during your travels. They will think of the worst case scenarios and tell you horror stories in a hope that you will listen and take precautions. Well make sure you do listen, and then put that information aside in a safe place where it won't bring about fear, but just may come to mind at an opportune moment of need. We are in this life for the experiences and learning through relationships, and the messages we're receiving within them is important. The people giving you warnings are in your life for a reason and that message may just be it.

If you're like me and believe that we are eternal beings and nothing can harm our true essence, even death, then you will put fear in its rightful place. It's a survival instinct. Most human beings recognise right action and you will know if you are endangering yourself. Trust that your instincts will alert you to possible dangers. Trust that you have put yourself in a position where the dangers will be no more than crossing the highway at home, but also believe that your needs will be met.

It's about trusting yourself and trusting in the Universe. Rehearse picking up on the right vibes before you leave home. Make decisions in your best interests, and those of others, based on those vibes. Trust that you recognise them and trust that the Universe is that all-knowing divine intelligence that leads you to the next 'point of attraction'- that next moment that drives your life in the direction of your making. Know that you're going to be able to adapt. Know that you're choosing to travel because it's something that you really want to do. Know that you're not going to put yourself into stupid situations and if you do that you'll make the right decisions to get out of them. Trust in the Universe that you will be in the right place at the right time.

I described my years of travel as my journey with the Universe. It was the Universe that was my travel companion. For years I had read New Age books about trust and believing in the ways of the Universe. Reading it, grasping it, believing it and then living it are all part of the process. Unless it really gels with you, you may not grasp the concept immediately here. But give it a chance and put it to the test. Trust that it will oblige.

My first noticeable instance of putting my trust to the test and receiving an 'instant' response to my requests was in early 2012, on my big trip. I met a great young German lady in the hostel I was staying at in Vancouver. She was travelling through Canada but also hadn't made any set plans. We saw a sign advertising a discounted bus pass for International Hostel card holders; it was a fifteen day, hop on hop off pass for the west and centre of Canada, incorporating Vancouver Island. It was a bargain and I trusted that the bus drivers would be able to negotiate the snow covered roads better than me. This was my first experience with wall to wall snow.

Now maybe I should have called this section, 'Careful What You Ask For' but when on a long stretch of our journey, we were aiming to reach Jasper and were destined to arrive at about 0230 hours. I said to myself, "I wish I didn't have my luggage to worry about at that time in the morning." The Universe more than obliged. At a connection along the way, our bags got put on the wrong bus after being assured that all was good for us to go off and grab a bite to eat. When we discovered that the bags were missing, the bus driver went out of his way to contact the driver of the bus that was carrying them. There was to be another changeover for the bags and he also rang the baggage handlers at that depot and rechecked at 11pm when it was all going down. We were lucky that this particular bus driver was stopping his shift at our destination and he promised to deliver the bags to our hostel the next morning. He drove way up through the ice and snow for us. Instead of becoming stressed about it in the beginning, I kept reminding myself to trust that the Universe was working it all out and I could get some sleep. **Not the way I would have done it, but that's the secret to letting go and trying not to control the 'how' of what's going to happen.**

Sometimes the Universe can provide the most basic of items that we require along the way and these can just show up and prove to you that you're being listened to. I decided that I wasn't going to buy many things along the way as I wanted my money to go towards travelling, accommodation and food. I decided I would let the Universe provide any other items that I really thought I would need or that I would like. Once at the snow-surrounded hostel in Jasper, Canada, I realised that I'd only brought along one of the two plain, long sleeved black T-shirts that I owned. I wished I'd brought the other one as well, as two would have been perfect for the layered ensemble that I was wearing each day. Within minutes of thinking this, I spotted an identical top hanging over the back of a chair. It was still there the next day and I asked everyone in the dorm if anyone there owned it. No one did. It had been left there from the weekend skiers. I washed it and claimed it. A perfect fit.

My German travel buddy had a couple of "sweet" knitted woollen hats and my beanie was a plain black one that could have belonged to a crab fisherman. I decided I would like a knitted hat to have something a bit more stylish. When I arrived at another friend's house in Colorado I walked in the door and she said, "There on the table, I knitted you a hat." It was beautiful and even more beautiful that the Universe was not only listening to me but also connecting with my special friends.

Next was a T-shirt. On my tour through Mexico I said to my roommate that all I needed now, with the weather getting warmer as I travelled south, was a nice T-shirt. On the last day of the tour we went out to Coco Bongos in Cancun and during some promotion for a local beer, a group of young ladies threw out black T-shirts. Guess who caught one. It fitted perfectly and looked great.

This continual beauty in the manner of the Universe convinced me to 'take my hands off the steering wheel' and to guide me towards my future. And that future would be extra special with a beautiful man. I decided I would trust the Universe whole-heartedly to lead me in the right direction of whatever it would be that would make me truly happy. With a partner or not. I didn't give it a list of requirements; just the result that I wanted – true happiness. Because sometimes we really don't know what or who will make us happy beyond belief. I'd spent all my life being proactive and making things happen and now it was time to really focus on the signs. I was wanting a life change but I still didn't know exactly how that change was going to look like, or if I would be on my own or with someone special.

I was sailing up around Lemnos in Greece and my next venture was to tour through Turkey but I was surprised with how hot it was. I decided I would look for another boat sailing around Turkey but none were available. It would be cooler out in the breeze on the ocean instead of touring on land. A friend of mine back in Australia said she was going to Malta and asked if I would be nearby. She missed me and would love to catch up. I told her that I was off to Turkey and maybe she could come there for a couple of days. We left it open. On one of my searches for a boat, I discovered a new feature on 'Find a Crew' that was a chat line. The only skipper online in the whole of the Mediterranean at that moment was my future husband, Thomas. I started up a conversation to try out the chat feature. He told me he was looking for crew to sail to Malta. Bells began ringing. He then suggested we have a Skype conversation. We did and he showed me around his beautiful boat. He was really sweet and I instantly liked him. We had a great chat for about forty minutes. As soon as I'd left the internet cafe I decided that I wanted to join Thomas in Spain and travel to Malta with him. I weighed the two places up in my mind: Spain versus Turkey, I hadn't been to either so each place would offer adventure. I would keep sailing and as a bonus, catch up with a dear friend. It would be nice to see a familiar face. The plan was that I would fly to Spain and then see my friend in Malta and then make my way back to Turkey at a later, cooler time. Then there were a few problems with communication. I'd booked my flight, sent Captain Thomas an email and then I got a message saying, "Are you coming still?" He obviously missed an email somewhere along the way. Well the rest is history. I jumped on board and haven't left. I haven't made it to Turkey yet but there is plenty of time for that. **The Universe has provided me with the most amazing opportunity to be happy and all I had to do was make the choice to say yes.**

When asking for something, try not to give the Universe too many details. We tend to confuse the issue. The end result is usually the only thing you need to ask for. The Universe will fill in the gaps. Trust it. It is amazing!!

Notes

Choices

Choose your love. Love your choice.

—Thomas S. Monson

BEFORE YOU DECIDE to go travelling you have many choices to make. There is your time-frame to work out and how that will be sustainable on your budget. There are choices to make about your budget and how you plan to save for your journey. Who will accompany you or will you travel alone? And of course there's your destination. Where are you going to go? What will you need to do before you go and what will you take? Answers to each of these choices will be entirely up to you but I aim to help you recognise some different options.

Firstly, you have to decide if you're really going to do it because it does cost money and you may have to make some compromises with your current lifestyle. You have to make a conscious choice that this is something you really want to do and recognise the benefits for the future. That may mean that you have to go without the latest phone and other fashion accessories or find alternative entertainment while you save. You may even have to put off owning a car or property for a while. By making this choice you're probably changing your mode of living from one of subsistence living to dream and inspirational living. You have something exciting and wonderful to look forward to. You will change the vibe in everything that you're doing.

If you're planning on a huge trip that will take years to save for, practice on smaller trips until the timing is right. Short holidays will help you put some of the ideas of this book into practice so that you can make the most of it at a later date. This book is about living in the now, not just about the big travel plans.

Fitting a big trip into your life's plan can be a bit awkward if you get too embedded in the daily demands of life. The more you get bogged down the more expectations people seem to have of you. Don't give up on your dreams of travel to fulfil someone else's dream. You need to be honest from the beginning with yourself and others that this is something you are going to do.

It's never too late to alter an unwanted direction of your life and make plans for travel. There's plenty of time to set your roots down somewhere. All throughout your life there will be opportunities for change and hopefully a journey will assist you in picking up on the vibe about when that change should be made. Travelling will help you identify your options and help you discover what truly brings you joy before you get trapped into thinking you can't change your circumstances. This is a true sense of freedom no matter where you are.

At the same time you don't have to wait until some catastrophe or life-altering event occurs before you head off on your adventure. Many people that I met along the way had had a relationship breakdown or a death in the family. These events tend to shake us up into examining our dreams, our mortality and we become determined to fulfil our life ambitions. Sometimes you just have to break free and make the decision to go before this occurs.

Once you've decided that you're serious about travelling you need to find out about the choices you have. Open your mind to discover the many options available. Reading travel stories from others will reveal a world of possibilities to you. You are only limited by your imagination and what others have accomplished already. You don't just have to travel to the regular destinations and do what everybody else is doing there. As you move around you will meet many people with just as many diverse approaches to travel. My goal here is to describe some of the options that I have either experienced myself or have heard from other people who are achieving their travel plans in interesting ways.

Very early in my travels when I was in Peru, I realised that I didn't want to just go back home to an ordinary life after my year of travel. I wanted to do something different and I was overwhelmed by the enormity of this decision. I had met some amazing people who had incorporated travel into the routine of their lives and I was amazed at the options.

There are a variety of alternatives to an 'ordinary' life that you can live. One man I met owned a summer ecolodge in Canada: he spent six months there; then spent 3 months exploring Canada and visiting friends; and the other quarter of the year immersing himself in a South or Central American country. He was loving and living to the maximum. Another young man I met was a professional gambler; his job took him everywhere and he embraced the culture of the people. An accountant I met, negotiated with his Sydney firm to have three months off a year as part of his conditions. An elderly couple I met in Stockholm owned an R.V., touring around Europe for half the year and storing it for the other half of the year while they lived in Melbourne. You don't have to slave your life away to be happy and fulfilled.

If it is volunteering that you are aiming for, there are many websites that help you organise a place to stay that will give you free board in exchange for your labour. I met many young people who were incorporating a month or so of volunteering into their travels. The type of work included farming on a community farm, child care at an orphanage, project manager in building a school and teaching English at a local school. These young people inspired me to plan something similar for the future. Websites that help you to organise volunteering are listed in the Appendix.

Another option is to use the website 'Find a Crew' or something similar, where you can find a boat to crew on for different periods of time. I had a summer sailing in the Mediterranean with some great yachts and then I met my husband on the last boat. He asked me to keep sailing around the world with him and that's where I currently am. You don't need a lot of experience to put your name down for this but you need to be willing to learn and cooperate in the confined space of a yacht. It pays to know a few recipes and be more than willing to clean and cook.

There are many young people working on private yachts all over the world too. You can find these paid opportunities on Find a Crew although some positions may require certain qualifications. I chose just to relax and contribute to the costs. At the most, this was 150 Euro a week for everything including drinks. It kept me well within my budget. Think of destinations such as The Caribbean, Madagascar, Mexico, The Mediterranean, The Whitsundays, Brazil, French Polynesia and Thailand and you will find available sailing vessels. The list of destinations goes on and you will surely be able to find one that appeals to you. I saw some great sights and met wonderful people while sailing through all the places I'd read about in history and in Greek mythology. I spent a year in the Caribbean and now I've just travelled through the South Pacific.

The captains of the boats were a wealth of knowledge. It was educational and entertaining. You can look at profiles on the website for free but I became a premier member when I was ready to look for a boat. This meant I could contact the captains directly. It was worth the fee as I only got in touch with people whose profile had been checked and I talked to the captains before I joined them. I later learned that the captains can get so many requests that they don't have time to answer each one individually. This can leave you wallowing in no man's land while you're trying to make plans so the membership is worthwhile considering. Each boat, except the last, had other people sharing the costs. It was a social and cultural exchange. You might ask why people would open their boats up to strangers. Many captains are looking for someone who is willing to share their journey and they are wanting to meet new people. Some are seeking assistance with a passage where they need extra hands to be on watch at night. They then repay by taking you to wonderful places. Living on a boat can be quite insulated if you don't actively engage in seeking out companionship.

When travelling on a long passage such as across the Pacific, I met several people who were swapping yachts along the way as they chose to take different or faster routes. There have been lots of captains seeking crew for different portions of their journey and you don't need to be on a website for this. Just visit the local yacht club or marina. As you may be alone with someone you don't know very well, it is a good idea to talk with them a few times before you join them and to let someone know the name of the boat and the owner. Cruising introduces you to many substantial people who are living their dreams and are experiencing extraordinary lives. I recommend it as a fulfilling option for travel.

Working in hostels as you travel is an option worth thinking of to help make your travel last longer. Most hostels offer free accommodation if you are willing to work for a few hours a day. This may give you more time in one place to learn more about the people, culture and visit more attractions.

Friends of mine have joined websites that help place you with everyday people in countries all over the world where you can work for your lodgings and food. They have had the most amazing adventures and built long lasting friendships. This is a great option for those older travellers who are unable to get work visas and want their travel to last multiple years. Be prepared to go that extra mile for your hosts and the Universe will ensure you are rewarded in many unexpected ways. A list of the websites they used is in the Appendix. When I researched these sites it made me want to try out some of the unique places. For a small joining fee, they will open a world of opportunity to you.

House sitting is available all over the world. If you have a love of animals and don't mind tinkering around someone's garden for a while, then this may be an option for you. People are finding that having their homes looked after by caring individuals or families is a much better option than leaving their pets in kennels or their house vacant while they are enjoying their own adventures. If you already own a home in a good position then you may consider house swapping as well.

Working for an exchange of lodgings is not just about saving money. It's about offering a part of yourself and your energy to someone who may really benefit from meeting you. It will help immerse you in the language and the culture. They will be able to offer lifetime memories and experiences that may lead you to future success and more joy. All participants will come away richer and wiser – even in challenging situations.

Some friends also use Share Ride sites instead of paying for hire cars on their own. So when you get to your destination check out if there is a share ride for where you want to go. On one occasion they searched for a ride to the Grand Canyon and got talking to someone offering a ride. They began to exchange details and worked out that they were standing right outside the hostel where their ride was. Serendipity is a wonderful thing. It's amazing how plans can work out so well. They were in the right place at the right time. They had a wonderful trip and remain friends with this person. Of course there are always risks involved so you need to be cautious and sensible. Pick up on the vibe and let your intuition guide you and always advise family of where you are and who you are going with.

If you are young and able to obtain a work visa for the country that you are planning on spending most of your time in, then you need to do this well in advance. Many of the job placement agencies will take a percentage of your wage and there may be hidden costs such as high lodging or travel fees that you may not have taken into account. If you are planning on working overseas to fulfil your travel dreams then make sure that it is the dream and not the work that is your priority. Try to line up your own work if possible.

The options I have listed above are usually fine for individuals but it is possible to include a journey with a young family also. Your needs will be different but there are still opportunities such as farm sitting or business sitting. Often husband and wife teams are needed so that people owning hospitality businesses can have a break without the huge expense of closing their business down for a while. There are many websites where you can register your interest or even begin your own business.

As you can see there are many diverse ways that can be utilised to plan your travel where you don't have to be at the mercy of the dollar for the length of your stay. You can combine some of these options and the key to do this is to plan. Unfortunately, you can't do that too far into the future as most captains, businesses or families will only be aware of their actual plans a few months in advance. Remain flexible and relaxed and be prepared for plan B.

Other choices to be made can be done by examining your driving force. What exactly is directing you towards travelling? Through reflection on this you are able to determine the priority of your destinations and what you might do once you're there.

Notes

Inspiration

If we were paid a dollar for every inspirational thought we ever had, we would all be rich beyond comparison. If every inspirational thought became a reality we would either be problem free or in grave danger.

—Gaylyn

"Inspiration comes from within yourself. One has to be positive. When you're positive, good things happen."

—Deep Roy

THEY SAY THAT success is 1% inspiration and 99% hard work but let's not ignore that one percent. It's inspiration that drives us to challenge ourselves and seek out new adventures. Inspiration could be an influential person, a story or a life-altering event. It's that catalyst that energises us into an action that leads us to growth and new experiences. By analysing your inspiration you will find that your trip will be more substantial because it will give you certain details to focus on and make it more meaningful to you. It's a way of personalising that well-worn landmark – making it unique for you. It's a way of living in the moment when you reach a particular destination and relishing in that moment of being there. No one around you, the weather or anything else can influence your joy of accomplishment because it is internal and totally in your control.

Try to recall the very first moment that you decided you wanted to travel to a particular destination and this will give you an insight into why you want to go there. Make a list of the activities you want to do as well as the sights that you want to see. What are the emotions that are stirred when you think about this place? Sometimes you may just need to sit in a café and to watch the people around you live their daily lives. Maybe it is climb the tallest peak and know that you're the highest person at that moment. Whatever it is, by examining your inspiration you will take the time to relish the ambience that the destination induces within you.

Travelling the world is more than ticking off a checklist or bucket list, although those are handy to have. It's about feeling those places and recognising how they change you or confirm something to you. By affirming that initial catalyst you are observing your journey's growth from the seed of inspiration.

My first inspiration for sailing around the world was when I was 10 watching the movie *The Dove*. It is a movie about a lone sailor circumnavigating the globe. I didn't want to sail around the world alone but the whole adventure captured my imagination. I thought at the time, "I'm going to do that one day." It was a long time before I began my journey but I never forgot that first inspiration. So when Thomas asked me to sail around the world with him, I had no hesitation in knowing that it was meant to be. Finding the catalyst will allow you to examine some long founded dreams that need to be followed through. This helps the experience to be all the more magical because it is fulfilling a dream. It's like coming through on a promise to yourself.

When you examine the true essence of your inspiration you will need to pay attention to detail to discover what it is that you need to accomplish when you get there. Ask yourself what it was that first thrilled you about that destination or activity. I know that my inspiration from watching *The Dove* was the vastness of the ocean, the sense of self-sustainability, the bravery of commanding a vessel through the elements and the sense of achievement that the captain felt. I was in awe of his accomplishments and was inspired to follow in his wake.

So as I'm travelling on our yacht I take notice of these things. On a clear day I wonder at the blue and relish the sense of feeling 'out there' away from everything. It has given me a sense of calmness about priorities in life by giving me time to examine what is truly important to me. Knowing that we are out there on our own has helped me to be self-reliant and trust in my own capabilities. In wild weather I have learnt to remain calm and seek unique solutions to issues that arise. Having travelled across the oceans has definitely given me a sense of achievement. We faced many trials and mishaps along the way that needed to be overcome. Achieving aspects of your dreams will give you a sense of accomplishment that you will carry throughout your life.

Once you analyse your inspiration, plan out the details. Identify clearly what it is you want to accomplish and why. Remove all barriers from your mind such as time restraints, cost and other responsibilities back home when you complete this activity, or you'll always find reasons that will complicate the matter. Identify the goals that you want to achieve while you're away. Once you have this mapped out you are ready to make a move to the next step and this is to plan or convince others around you to join you.

Understanding your dreams and being able to verbalise them will help partners and friends know how important they are to you. You can become an inspiration for those wanting to join you on this voyage if you're looking for company. It helps them to grasp your intentions and if you are exact with your reasoning they probably won't try and take over the journey. It may also become a dream of theirs to fulfil.

By fulfilling your dreams you are walking your talk and strengthening your credibility as a person. This helps to follow through on your other ambitions in life. When you realise you have the strength to do something as bold and brave as to travel you can accomplish many things. (Just because lots of people do it doesn't mean that you're not brave). It helps build confidence in finding the necessary skills to keep you well and safe throughout life. Believe in yourself and your dreams.

Notes

Growth

Growth is never by mere chance; it is the result of forces working together.

—James Cash Penney

NOW THE TYPE of growth I'm referring to here is not the type you might get between your toes from using a communal shower. It's about the personal growth and how that will affect your relationships during your journey and when you get back home. Before you even leave your country it is important to acknowledge that you will have different and more defined options and attitudes after your journey. Your travel will change your relationship with your peers, your family and with yourself. These changes will occur on at least three different levels; there is the internal level of self-discovery and acknowledgement; then there is the level of defining and improving your interpersonal relationships in a way that you aim for everyone to benefit; and lastly, is the level of projecting your wants and desires into the future to shape your own life.

The amount of self-reflection and change required will depend on how ego-centric you are before you leave. If the world has mainly revolved around you at home and people have pampered to your every whim – by the way, it is unlikely that you will recognise that this is you because you probably think you are still hard done by – then you will have the greatest room for growth through this experience. If you are the type of person who embraces change and sees it as a challenge and adventure, then this transformation will be a more natural evolution.

Firstly, and most importantly, it is the change in the relationship with yourself that you need to acknowledge. You are likely to be at a stage in your life where you are wanting to define yourself as an adult human being. There is no better rite of passage than to under go a trip of a lifetime. Not only will it make you take responsibilities like you may never have had to before, but it also gives everybody back home the space and time away from you, so long-held personal behaviours can alter. Changing before someone's eyes is a difficult thing for many to comprehend and this travel will give you the time and space to initiate the types of changes that you may deem necessary for a successful life.

It isn't just your upbringing at home that has helped to shape who you are as a human being, although psychologists will claim it is the most important component. School with its challenges and successes will have contributed to the process quite considerably. Unfortunately not everyone has necessarily had a smooth path through school and the social mine field that surrounds this institution. Hopefully you will be able to reflect on your schooling with some form of affection in years to come, if not immediately after leaving, or acknowledge the resilience you have developed as a result of a tough ride. The messages that you received from particular teachers can ultimately shape the qualities that were identified, and encourage or discourage you to have certain beliefs about yourself and determine your self-confidence or your drive to prove them wrong.

One of the most difficult challenges you will probably ever face is to identify your strengths and faults and go about determining how to make any changes that you wish to. It seems almost humanly impossible to change your inner responses to certain stimuli but there are strategies available; meditation and reflection with an added mix of willpower are involved. After a conflict you might say to yourself that you'll never act that way again only to find yourself in similar circumstances at another time and you react almost the same way. Many people believe that a 'leopard can't change its spots' but that's not true. It is our internal reaction mechanisms that we need to examine to enable us to make the alterations desired.

One of the easiest methods of adopting change in this sphere is to take more note of the vibes around you in different situations and act accordingly. It's the 'act accordingly' that is the major hurdle as reading the vibe is just a matter of focusing on what is going on around you. An undeniable way of ensuring you are making the right choice about how to act is to ask yourself, 'Am I doing this for self-gain at the detriment of others or am I doing this in the best interests of everyone involved?' If you are aiming for a 'win-win' situation then you are likely creating a good choice. As you learn to do this more often, you will change your general behaviour and thought patterns to aim for this intuitively.

Other than the advice given here, inner growth and change is a topic best dealt with in another volume, but I will recommend that you read 'Search Inside Yourself' by Google's self-proclaimed 'Jolly Good fellow,' Chade-Meng Tan. I personally utilise the strategies described and they are gentle and enjoyable. As you will have time to meditate when waiting for buses, trains and planes you will be able to focus on personal growth and developing inner peace.

Networking and building ideas and solutions utilising different people's strengths is becoming more of the model of success on a grand scale rather than individual competitiveness. Seeking what you want out of life and focusing on your own ambitions is still encouraged, yet there is an obvious shift occurring to a more collaborative way of working. We are told constantly that it's a "dog-eat-dog" world full of competition, although working with others appears to be the major way of developing our skills, wealth and joy. This synchronising strategy appears to be leading the way, rather than stepping all over someone else to get our needs met. Sharing ideas and contacts generates a whole new world of opportunities. You can raise your own and other people's level of energy and the whole vibe of a situation when you share a certain passion and show an interest in what's been said. Interpersonal relationships are becoming more and more complex and even more important for our success. Travelling introduces you to opportunities to meet the people who could be sharing driving your future.

Managing our time and relationships is becoming a blur as social media can be eating up our precious personal time. Even though you may be seeing your interactions on social media as being vital for maintaining your contacts, it might not be the best way to have quality relationships. It is unbelievable the amount of people who just hang out on their phones when travelling instead of getting lost in the moment in the beautiful places they're visiting. It seems to be more paramount to share what they're doing rather than experiencing it for themselves. Be careful not to fall into this trap. Keeping your posts up to date may be important to you but not as important as enjoying the moment. You may discover that you don't have an option to get online in many remote places and hopefully you'll enjoy the break.

When you're travelling, focus on the people around you and the messages and opportunities that come your way. Pick up on the vibe. Recognise what you have to offer someone in the way of advice, talents and ideas. Sharing information helps others to determine possible avenues for themselves. You may even meet someone who will later become vital in a career option. You will meet people of all ages and from all walks of life who have a wealth of knowledge and experience to share. Remain open and gravitate to a range of different types of people. You will probably develop relationships with the most unusual candidates who will enlighten you.

Not only will you have opportunities to meet new people but you'll have the opportunity to reflect on the relationships back home. I'm a firm believer of not dumping people just because they're not meeting your expectations or needs or that they're acting a bit toxic. Certainly you need to be wise about where your energy will flow when it comes to friendships, but sometimes people need to be sent a bit of love and light when they're stepping on the wrong path. You can keep your distance without discarding people altogether. You can always say no to people if they're asking you to do something you don't want to. And if you don't know how to say no to some people – learn to do. Be kind to them and yourself. You can take a backseat without deserting them altogether. The roles could be reversed sometime down the track. These people are in your life for a reason. It's time to reflect on all your relationships, with parents, siblings and friends.

This space gives you time to decide how you want these relationships to progress. How can they be enjoyable and beneficial to everyone? If there are aspects of these relationships that have been dysfunctional, now is the time to set about change. You can decide how you want these relationships to develop in the future then make sure your actions reflect those wishes.

Some people know how to push your buttons to get a reaction. Modify your reactions so they can't change your vibrations. They will soon get the message that they no longer have the remote control and adjust their behaviour when interacting with you.

Projecting wants and desires into the future is about shaping who you are now and opening your mind to possibilities. As The Rolling Stones sing, 'You can't always get want you want,' but you can give it a good try. Sometimes what we think we want isn't what is best for us and the Universe seems to have us dodging what we're striving for. The road can seem quite difficult and you'll probably pick up on the vibe – just not feeling right. There are three reasons why this may be occurring. The first and biggest obstacle is that the timing just may not be right for you and there are other things to learn. Secondly, you have to work hard for it so you'll appreciate it more and thirdly, you're just not meant to have it. Having said that, we are in charge of our own destiny and we need to make sure we're shaping ourselves and our future for positive gain and interactions. By behaving in a positive enthusiastic manner, you will draw like-minded people towards you who will play a role in your life. The same works when you have a self-defeating attitude. It's the law of attraction. What you are giving most of your attention to, will come your way – positive or not.

If you haven't already seen or read anything about **The Secret**, now is the time to view this documentary. It encompasses most of what I have thought for many years and it spells it out very clearly. You are in charge of picking up on the vibes, attracting what you are focusing on and moving your own life forward.

My main point here is for you to recognise that travelling away from familiar surroundings and relationships gives you the best prospect to make changes. Take advantage of this opportunity for growth. It is more difficult once you get back home and it is easy to fall back into old patterns. Ensure you learn some strategies to avoid this occurring and project the person you want to be.

Notes

Communication

A wonderful fact to reflect upon, that every human creature is constituted to be that profound secret and mystery to every other.

—Charles Dickens, A Tale of Two Cities

COMMUNICATION IS THE tool that turns growth into a recognisable accomplishment and helps us to unlock the mystery of ourselves and others. Being in touch through self-talk and being honest with yourself helps to identify why you are wanting to take this particular journey and assists you in acknowledging your learning. Genuine communication with others throughout your journey offers the opportunity to make real and worthwhile connections and keep relationships alive and thriving back home. Keeping that communication positive is building solid foundations for future happiness.

Positive self-talk is paramount for moving towards the point of attraction. This creates the vibe where 'magic' seems to happen. Amazing coincidences and opportunities appear to arrive in a timely manner. Be kind to yourself and avoid being judgemental other than to note that a change of behaviour may be necessary to attract your desires into your life. Reflections can occur through meta-cognition — thinking about your thinking or through automatic writing in a journal. Just write anything that comes to your mind and then steer it towards affirmations. Your stance will reflect your confidence and you will attract positive and fun people into your life.

Mostly, I would keep a journal by writing just one entry per town or place visited. I didn't want to make it a burden by trying to write every day. I know that suits some people and you need to do whatever works for you and is manageable. I'm not artistically creative but I saw some beautiful examples of other traveller's journals, with small sketches and colourful borders. I remember being fascinated by an old journal that was made into a children's book and it was full of old tickets, postcards and insights. It was a beautiful memento for the person's descendants and something to enjoy and reflect on. I was drawn to England many years ago because of wanting to investigate my past lives so I decided to keep a journal of all the spirits that contacted me there. I wrote about kings and queens in the castles in Wales, soldiers on the battlefields and ordinary folk walking the walls of different cities. I enjoyed writing it and it made me really concentrate and connect with spirits at this time. I love to go back through it and remember my connections from that time. Sometimes it feels like it was another person who wrote it. There are such wonderful messages that I forget over time. It is nice to revisit them.

Now, that I'm travelling all the time, I keep a blog. I try and write about the funny little things that make me laugh along the way. I want to entertain my friends and family, record my stories for later and inspire people to travel and follow their dreams. Think of your audience and what your purpose will be but keep track of those wonderful little stories. There will be so many of them.

Keeping your relationships growing back home while you're away will take a little bit of an effort. A friendly postcard or a fun email that describes a funny story will increase the vibes around those relationships. Good thoughts for your safety and hoping that you're having an awesome time from those loved ones increases your vibe. The Universe will pick up on all of these energies and where people's thoughts are focused.

Before leaving home it may pay to purchase an unlocked mobile phone. You don't need anything fancy – just a straightforward phone will do. If you are in a country for a long time, then you can obtain a local SIM for a small outlay. This will enable people back home to contact you in an emergency. You may also use it to ring overseas by using a call card in addition. In these cases, you just ring a local number. Call cards come in a lot of varieties and you may need to shop around in each country. Usually, small little corner shops will sell a range of these. There will be cheaper calls on offer to those countries where a lot of local immigrants have come from. You can use these call cards in public phone booths as well but finding a functioning one may be a challenge. If you've bought a SIM with data then using an online phone line can be a great inexpensive option.

Take care if you decide to use International Roaming services. These can be very expensive and many a traveller has come unstuck with the resulting phone bill from using too much data. Many phone companies alert their customers to high data usage nowadays but, just because Facebook was free on your phone deal in your home country doesn't mean it's free on International Roaming. Emailing is the best and most inexpensive method of keeping in touch although it can sometimes drive you crazy trying to find good internet.

Emailing can be done at your own leisure and you don't have to worry about time zone differences. Face to face methods of communication online tend to require good internet and that isn't always possible. It's certainly a good way for family members to see that you're still in one piece and that you haven't gone too crazy with new tattoos. Come to think of it maybe limit these calls if you have gone crazy on a tattoo and piercing blitz. Whatever you do, try not to spend too much time on calls back home. You are there to enjoy the vibe of the moment of where you are. There will be plenty of locals to connect with for a chat.

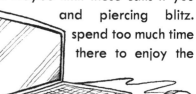

Speaking at least some basic greetings and requests for information in the language of the land where you're visiting is helpful and courteous. Humans have a great way of getting their needs met through hand signals and body language as well. It is difficult to learn lots of different languages if you're doing some world travels but a bit of Spanish and French come in handy in a lot of countries. Just research on the internet and print off some basic sayings if you're not taking a translator or dictionary with you. There are many places that will offer inexpensive language courses. For example, you can participate in an intense course of Spanish for a month for under US$500 in many South American countries. It's a great opportunity if you are planning on staying in one spot for a while. I have met people who have done one of these courses and they were communicating fluently with the locals.

You will find that some locals will want to practise English with you so remember to speak clearly and encourage them in their efforts. You will find children particularly willing and will rush up to you and try their English out. Many will use their limited English in the first greeting. Don't let that stop you. Young people will most often recognise famous people's names. Introduce yourself or name them as someone famous to have a good laugh with them. Sing a song with them and dance in the street. They will usually be up to speed with the latest hits. Smaller children will often recognise the tune to a nursery rhyme and will be happy to sing it to you in their own language. Interacting with the youth of a country can be a real joy. There are usually lots of laughs and big smiles. You'll walk away feeling good.

If you already speak the same language do not be shy about beginning conversations. Ask questions about your locality. People are generally polite and proud of their homeland and are flattered that you've travelled to visit it. They love to share and they will know a lot of places to visit. I have been amazed with the kind of assistance offered to me in new countries. In Greece a captain and I were offered a moped to borrow because it was too hot to walk to the bus terminal and earlier a fisherman had brought us some of his catch. People have escorted me to a sought after destination or offered me meals or a place to stay. **People are amazing.**

I have only once had a negative experience and that was in Niagara Falls when I asked a lady the way to the Greyhound bus terminal. She turned with her hands on her hips and said, "What do I look like, a tourist bureau?" I was thankfully quick-witted that day and responded with, "No, I thought you looked like a polite person but I was mistaken." I found my own way to the bus terminal. It was a painless experience and made an interesting moment to reflect upon. I didn't know what else had happened in the poor woman's life that day so I didn't judge her, but I took a mental note that maybe was the only negative interaction I had on my journey. And it wasn't so bad.

You will usually find that your interactions will be positive because there are so many positive people out there. I don't understand why there is so much conflict in the world when people are generally fantastic. It just doesn't make sense. The mass consciousness of the people needs to reflect this inner beauty, not the hatred that can be brought about by a lack of tolerance for difference. As a traveller, you are sharing the joy of being human. **Make a local person's day through kindness, inquisitiveness and peace.**

You will meet some of the most amazing people when you are travelling but every now and then there will be someone who will just rub you the wrong way. Learn to walk away and not worry about them or their attitude. If you let them get the better of you, you can sometimes react in a way that will make you feel bad later on. How you conduct yourself in a conversation will give people an overall feel for what sort of person you are. Be open and listen to other people's truths. You gain no energy by trying to change their way of thinking, you only drain yourself. When listening, remember to focus on what the person is saying and ask questions that don't belittle what they think or make them think that you don't value what they believe in. Instead of making a judgement, try to understand why they may have a different perspective from you. Remember that you have no right to take someone else's peace away from them. If you're adding to their life in a positive way then you are leaving them feeling uplifted, happy and appreciated. Focus your energy on others during group discussions and you'll find you'll get so much more out of these times by lifting the vibe. People always need to feel valued. Help to leave a positive image by being polite, fun and helpful. You may even find that you have a lot in common and decide to continue part of your journey with them following a common theme.

Notes

Themes

Some broad themes brought me where I am today. At a very young age, my hobby became thinking and finding connections.

—Dean Kamen

IT IS FUN to think of a bit of a theme to follow at different times during your travels. If you did it all the time it would be a bit tedious and restrictive, and that's the last thing that you want, but on occasions it is exciting. If you can picture the different things that you want to do along the way other than just visiting a place in relation to a theme, it will help you to plan.

Identify an area of culture that you love such as art, dance, music or architecture and find out about the opportunities to visit particular places that display unique examples of these. The types of themes I have met other travellers following have included festivals, opportunities to volunteer, the wonders of the world – ancient, modern and natural, history, military battlefields, ghost tours, natural phenomena, literacy tours and plenty who have shopping as their main theme. Picking a theme is a great way to get like-minded people on board with your journey if you're looking for company.

If you are involved in a club of some sort you may be able to encourage some other members along. Sometimes you can incorporate sport or hobbies such as golf or archery. Diving is a popular theme as dive spots can vary so greatly all over the planet. You have many options to include others in a themed adventure.

Literary tours are becoming more available all over the world. Visiting a place where a particular movie or book was located brings your experiences with them to life. It's a wonderful thing to be able to picture the images in your own mind as the author or script writer may have done. It can deepen your appreciation for the plot if you're actually there. I remember visiting Bath in England many years ago and being captivated by the romance of the dance and tea houses where the action of many of Jane Austin's novels took place. Also visiting a destination that is referred to in many different movies and books such as London Tower or Central Park brings fiction into reality. It helps you to pick up on the vibe in the book. Later you can appreciate watching or reading about these destinations with recollection of detail.

Some places lend themselves to particular themes. For instance, Colombia and New Zealand have great opportunities for extreme sport along with many other outdoor activities such as hiking or bike riding. Colombia has three ranges of the Andes running through it meaning that there are plenty of mountains and valleys for climbing, caving, abseiling and rafting. You also have a chance to visit a section of the Amazon there. Activities are inexpensive and the scenery is magnificent. New Zealand also has a diverse range of lush and unique landscapes worthy of being a breathtaking backdrop for extreme sports, although the costs are a bit higher there but at the time of writing, they do have a national insurance to cover visitors who are involved in accidents.

Often you learn more about a place once you get there and what possible themes are available.

I was lucky enough in Budapest to be told about a very inexpensive classical concert to go to and in Barcelona I found out about a crazy famous architect, Antoni Gaudi, who built bizarre houses that everyone else had heard about but me. You can't know everything before you leave but by talking to people along the way you will find little treasures that aren't always in the guide books. Building this base of themes improves your general knowledge and allows you to find out more about yourself and certainly your world. You'll find things that you like and do not like about different examples of the above, or you might just love everything that is a little bit new and different and this in itself is an insight.

When we were leaving the Mediterranean to cross the Atlantic on the sailing vessel, Qi, at the end of 2012, we were met by a pod of dolphins before the morning light. Thomas woke me up to watch a display of these playful mammals racing and jumping through luminous plankton. It was a psychedelic scene. The dolphins were lit up by the plankton and you could see all of their features. The streak in the water left by them rocketing through and playing in our wash was reminiscent of comets. As they leapt in the air their splashes were lit up and fell like they were in slow motion. If I hadn't witnessed this spectacle first hand, I would never have believed it. Had I known that the phenomenon existed, I would have put it on my bucket list. It confirmed that there truly is magic in the world. Sometimes we have to really make an effort to seek out life-altering experiences and other times they just cross our path. Now I have learned that this luminous plankton is in an abundance in certain parts of the globe. It would be great to adopt a theme around visiting these destinations.

In 2001 I had a journey to Europe based on working there and discovering the relevance of some past lives that I had recalled during a regression some years beforehand. Lessons from past lives can be put together to work out patterns of behaviour. These patterns can be recognised and you can adjust your behaviour accordingly to break any negative and repetitive actions. My journey led me to castles in Conwy in northern Wales and the chalets in the Loire Valley in France. The big messages I worked out were to push any fear of death aside and to understand the continued cycle of life and existence for myself and my loved ones. Having just lost my father the year before, I found this realisation very comforting. Our inner being, our light, our soul, this divine intelligence will never fade. It will always be who we truly are. It also made me more determined to tackle my other existing fears to see if I could avoid taking them into any future lives.

During this extended trip away I kept a travel journal with a difference. I wrote about the different spirits that I encountered at the various destinations. Writing these interactions made for great reading at a later date. I've included a meditation here that will assist those of you in reaching your past lives to make this a theme for your journey. Automatic writing is another method that I use.

Tip Box

Past-life Regression Meditation

Make yourself comfortable lying down in a beautiful room, a park or in the rainforest.

Begin with your toes and imagine socks of bubbles gliding onto your feet and moving all the way up your body.

As this sock stretches out it becomes one bubble protecting you and sealing you from outside forces. Change the colour of that bubble from clear to purple to red to blue to orange to pink, (in no particular order).

Try and poke that bubble and watch as it flexes because you have made it so strong.

Choose one of the colours to stay with you throughout your journey. Examine this colour, its hue and texture. Colour choices have meaning and we will explore this at a later time. Your colour choice could be significant.

This bubble will travel and flex with you as you travel in the past to old lives.

Travel now, fly, walk or ride to a meadow. At the end of this meadow is a stream with a waterfall.

In amongst the waterfall, as if it's a part of it, is a castle built into the rocky cliff. Vines with flowers are interlaced through the rocks and bricks.

You move through the front archway. Here you are faced with a number of doors.

One is a solid wooden door with wrought iron decorations, another is green of medium strength, and another door is white and sheer, so light that it moves with the wind like a curtain. You can see movement beyond it.

Check on your bubble once more and then move through one of the doors.

Here someone greets you and offers to take you on a journey with them. They begin to tell you things about who you were. Listen to what they say until you can picture the person they are describing.

Take note to see where you are being lead to in the world. See the sights around, note the smells and the energies. Remember that you are an outsider looking in and that you can leave at any time. You are in control of your journey. Once you have learned about the time and place ask questions about your purpose for living that life. Ask what lessons you learned and how you made a difference in the world. Ask what was left undone.

With even more questions than when you arrived you realise that the sun is setting and it is time to return. Take your journey in reverse.

Once you've returned to where your journey began give thanks to the person who showed you the way. Know that you can always return to that door or return into the valley and try a different door.

(If the life was a difficult and distressing one you can know that you are safe now and there is nothing to fear where you are now. Learn from that life and take those lessons with you into the future)

Tip Box

Automatic writing

Make sure you're in a comfortable peaceful zone. Prepare yourself with a writing book, a pen or a pencil and just begin to write. Let your imagination wander and write about where it's taking you. Try and write a poem or just prose when you enter this relaxed zone. The important thing is to not hesitate with spelling or punctuation. Get your thoughts down and see what you come up with. I have been amazed at some of the words I have used. I've had to look some of them up in the dictionary and I'd used them correctly—freaky.

Exploring the official Wonders of the World has often been the theme for travellers I have encountered. At some point during their journey they ensure they visit a nearby world wonder but don't let the theme be the total mission.

Others have made missionary work or volunteering their theme. Each of these will offer incredible opportunities to mix with the locals. Others choose more self-indulgent themes such as exploring culinary delights. Whatever theme you choose, ensure it resonates with you because then you'll know you're on the right track. I will ask you to add your unique and original ideas for themes to my website to assist others in creating memorable journeys.

Notes

Destinations

WHERE EXACTLY YOU go is truly of little consequence, the important thing is that your journey takes you to places that matter to you. What you will discover is that the world is full of amazing stunning places. It is impossible to identify a favourite country from my years of travel. They each have something interesting and beautiful to offer and each has some quirky ways of life that differ from yours back home that will make you wish for similar surroundings on some occasions. So this chapter will outlay a few options for the types of destinations that you might be seeking. This is based on experience and there are still many places that should be researched to find other options will personally suit you. If you are on a world tour then there will be a range of locations that you will want to see. Pacing yourself with busy sightseeing

ANYWHERE 112 KM
EVERYWHERE 320 KM
SOMEWHERE 105 KM
NOWHERE 30 KM

combined with relaxing getaways will give your mind and your body time to reflect and recuperate as you go. Pace yourself and take in the unique vibe of each of your destinations.

Probably the most incredible sightseeing that I have ever done was in Egypt and Europe. Seeing the ancient ruins that have been excavated from their graves in the deserts of Egypt was a thrilling experience. Each of the temples revealed a different aspect into the lives of the people who once existed in these civilisations. It was like a journey back in time and an insight to where some basic lessons in humanity were first described. The temples were a symbol of their incredible dedication to their gods and spiritualism. This kind of devotion is also reflected throughout the cities of Europe. Whether or not you are religious yourself, doesn't take away the appreciation that the magnificent cathedrals of Europe inspire. Any historical landmark is more than a pile of stones as you wonder at the complexities of the lives of the inhabitants and appreciate their accomplishments with limited tools. You will find a true fascination and respect for their ways and a sincere gratefulness for the emotional evolution that societies have undertaken as you journey through historic sites.

Seeking out natural wonders along your journey won't be difficult and will help you to develop an appreciation for the power of Mother Nature. You will also learn to appreciate her sense of humour too as you discover the unique and the bizarre. Many countries claim to have the biggest, tallest or longest something. The Galapagos Islands was one of these types of destinations. Volcanic activity had caused many long lava tunnels. We arrived at one which claimed to be the 'second' longest in the world. Later when I was reading a brochure I discovered the first longest was only a few kilometres away. In Colombia they claim to have the second biggest canyon in the world where you can paraglide for a very reasonable cost. Sailing the Caribbean and the South Pacific offers such beautiful sunsets and scenery that you begin to wonder why everyone isn't there. The South Island of New Zealand is one of the most jaw-dropping scenic places you could discover along with Scandinavia. The frozen landscape of a Canadian winter is magical and watching an active volcano in Central America spit fire and ash is exhilarating. No matter where you go you should be able to find places of natural beauty that amaze you.

Lazy coastal destinations where you can recoup and take stock of your journey and your life can range from isolated walk-in camping spots in Colombia with jungle-trimmed beaches, to all-inclusive hotels in Jamaica and Mexico that have organised entertainment. Some beach camping grounds have net covered hammocks under a communal waterproof gazebo open to the air such as in Tayrona Park. So camping equipment isn't necessarily an issue. Surfing is rife in many Caribbean islands and inexpensive accommodation can be found at the beaches of Peru or Bali. You will   always be able to find like-minded people to chill out with and assist in enjoying the vibe of a beach location.

If you are wanting to get away from civilisation and the demands of an ordinary life then the Pacific Islands are certainly an option and sailing is a great way to get there. You just need to investigate the usual routes taken and the time of the year that they are travelled to plan your cruising. You don't need to own a yacht or even have money for your fare as there are many cruisers looking for crew to assist them with their passages. Experienced or not. Sailing is a magnificent way to be self-reliant and to set your personal challenges. Trusting in your boat, your captain and especially your own capabilities, builds an inner strength that will guide you through life.

Wherever you choose to travel ensure it is to a place that you are drawn to in some sort of way. This is a type of energy the Universe is using to drive you towards certain lessons and growth. They don't always need to be positive experiences at the time but you will find that through reflection, you will find the lessons that you need to learn at that time. The most respectful thing you can do towards yourself is to learn those lessons and enjoy your moments at that destination.

Notes

Companions

"She was struck by the simple truth that sometimes the most ordinary things could be made extraordinary, simply by doing them with the right people..."

—Nicholas Sparks, *The Lucky One*

PERSONALLY, I LOVE to travel on my own and if you're not in a relationship then there is nothing like the sense of freedom that comes from being totally in control of your own decisions. If you are in a relationship and you want this relationship to continue then your partner back home might tire of hearing about the super cool people you're meeting along the way if they don't join you. You might have to consider insisting that they come along. People tend to gravitate towards a lone traveller very quickly and you are rarely on your own. I got to meet lots of other lone travellers along my way who struck up many interesting conversations. I often found people who would join me on small sections of my tour. I really enjoyed the odd bit of extended company along the way especially because being so far from home I wasn't seeing a trusted familiar face for a while. Sometimes these people enter your life only for a short time to teach you some lessons along the way; sometimes they leave forever; or sometimes they keep in touch and become lifelong friends. If you do decide to travel with someone it is imperative that you have clear expectations from the beginning about how you want your journey to go.

If you decide to travel with a buddy then it is important to choose someone who you respect and they respect you. There will be times when you want to go in separate directions purely because of personal interest and you will want some 'alone time'. A person who respects you won't get cranky at you because you want to do this. They won't take it personally and will enjoy their own space. Privacy and quiet time become important when doing a lot of travel and this person must respect both. Having shared dreams about certain places will help planning. It is a good idea to book a few concrete flights or bus tours to ensure that you won't be talked out of doing something special for yourself because your travel buddy has decided to gravitate towards something new that wasn't on the agenda. Lots of discussions about expectations before travelling can help avoid conflict along the way and issues should be discussed candidly. Choose someone who shares the same sort of sense of humour as you. That's a good measuring stick. Don't rule out travelling with siblings or parents even if they're not currently your favourite people. It opens up a whole new dimension to your relationship and gives you wonderful shared memories. I have had many wonderful trips with my mum and I love that we have those journeys to talk about when we get together.

Some of the types of issues you might have to discuss are: borrowing money from each other, expectations on who's paying entry fees. How do you feel about sharing items? What are the expectations when you go for an evening out? What happens if one of you gets sick or injured and what happens if one of you falls in love along the way? Whenever I travelled with my mum we would always borrow money off each other so we didn't have to run to an ATM if we saw something that we wanted to buy. We kept track in a little notebook and at the end of each trip we would settle things. It was often only a few dollars here and there that needed to be exchanged as we both helped each other out evenly. But not everyone is so conscientious about paying debts, so take care. If your buddy always lets you pay for the coffee back home, there's a good chance that he or she will be hitting you up for more than that when you're travelling. Agree to keep tabs on any financial exchanges. Many a good friendship has ended over one or both individuals thinking that the other was mooching off them.

So, girls in particular, it's a great idea if you can share items such as hair dryers or computers as it cuts down on your luggage, but sharing clothing or make up can become an issue. Getting to a laundry can be a hassle so you might miss out on wearing your favourite top because your buddy wore it last and people can have different usage expectations with makeup. Just saying...talk about it before you leave home. You might not think it important but sometimes the little things can irk you more when you're away from your home space. Boys are less likely to worry too much as they can usually get by with a lot less items but always borrowing your mate's hair gel or shaving cream could make you become unpopular too.

Whenever you plan a big night out make sure that you keep an eye on each other and check in with each other if you end up talking to different groups of people. It is never cool to leave a venue without your mate or without your mate knowing that you're leaving and where you're going. Don't go home without letting him or her know where you are! Make sure each other's expectations are clear.

Unfortunately the strain of travelling long haul flights and rushing to catch buses can tax the body and one of you could end up unwell or suffer an injury along the way. You need to share your travel insurance details with each other and make sure you have chosen a company that will look after both of you if you need to fly home. It is not unusual to find an insurance cover that will look after your travel buddy as well as the sick or injured person, but it needs to be stated at the outset of the journey. Sometimes an extra couple of nights' stay in one spot is all that is needed to rest up and get well again. Make sure you build this flexibility into any long term travel plans because undoubtedly one of you will get a fever sometime over an extended journey. It also raises the question about whether to pull the plug on the whole journey and think about doing the trip at another time. Your health is important, so you might need to make a tough decision. Decide before you leave if it is an option for one to continue on without the other. When you are unwell and away from home it can be quite miserable so make sure your buddy is well cared for before you decide to continue on your way.

Then there's the big whammy. What are you going to do if one of you finds the love of your life? Does one become the third wheel? Do you promise to stick together no matter what? Do you feel happy for your friend and look for a new buddy if they decide to join their new love on their travels? Now if you've fallen in love with each other, then that's fine, but otherwise you need to discuss this topic before you leave home and be realistic. You won't want to give up the opportunity to be with someone special if the feelings are that strong. If you are travelling for a long time, there is a very good chance that at least one of you will find romance along the way. One solution may be to do a bit of solo travelling for a short while but agree to meet up again soon along the way. It's nice to give people a bit of space to lose themselves in a romance but you don't want to be left hung out to dry either. Have a plan and then be flexible.

Sometimes travel buddies have a break up themselves. Have the conversation about what might happen if your relationship comes to an end on the journey. It wouldn't be the first time that it's happened.

I'd made up my mind that I really wanted to test out my skills travelling alone on my year off. I didn't want to compromise with anyone or even have a discussion about what I wanted to do. I just wanted to make the arrangements and do it. I longed to see if I could truly trust the Universe as much as my spiritual lessons had convinced me to do. So on my big journey, my travel companions were myself and the Universe, so I felt I was never alone. This is because I consider the Universe to be the collection of all the souls, earthly or not.

Now that I am in a wonderful travelling relationship with the captain of Qi, I am finding the joys of sharing my experiences with someone I love. I have had to wait a long time before meeting someone with similar interests and energy levels as myself. Our first time on land together was a journey back to Germany to meet his family and to get out of the hurricane season for a few weeks. We stayed with his sister in the woods near Hamburg and had the most wonderful time; walking the dogs, going to archery, accompanying his friends and family to different events. We became even closer and learned a lot about ourselves. When we returned to the boat we planned a month tour on land around Colombia. It was one of the best trips of my life. He is so flexible and adjusts so well socially to change that I felt relaxed throughout the journey. I can't believe that I fell in love with such a wonderful person who is also a great travelling buddy. I wish the same for you if that is what your heart desires.

Anyone who is prone to panic and paranoia should be left on the tarmac along with anyone who is bossy and domineering. Even if it is someone you love dearly. You want to be able to 'feel' and 'live' this travel experience. You need to be in charge of yourself.

HE WAS SO WORRIED AND PANICKY THAT HE'D LEFT SOMETHING BEHIND THAT HIS TRAVEL BUDDY LEFT HIM BEHIND

In all honesty, there are plenty of people to leave behind. Some people get caught up in the excitement of someone else's dreams and claim that they identify with them and want to jump on board. I was once roped into believing people who said they wanted to travel with me but they showed no indication of preparing for the journey. They weren't on the same page as me and it took way too long to work that out. For me and them. Don't wait for them. Set them a time limit to prepare, do your preparation and plan to go with or without them. Travelling on your own opens up a whole world of different opportunities.

As I said before, you won't be alone for long but you will have a variety of travel companions along the way. It's an exciting way to travel and a way that you can learn a lot about yourself. You can get to enjoy your own company and be totally responsible for all your arrangements. There is no one else to blame for mistakes made and that's a good life lesson in itself. Too many people find fault in their childhood or circumstance where they can blame others, and this type of attitude only perpetuates ongoing bad behaviour cycles within relationships. Learning to take full responsibility helps to break these cycles. You also become accustomed to not being able to run away from yourself so you can really study the human being that you are. You will also have the freedom to make changes to who you are. While no one who knows you or has past expectations of you is around, it is the perfect time to try new patterns of behaviour that you would like to adopt. Decide on the aspects of your personality that you're proud of and stick with these. Those little demons that we all have – work on them and see if you can go home happier with the person you've become. By the time you get home these behaviours will hopefully naturally occur and be easy to maintain. Try hard not to fall into old patterns of behaviour once back in normal routines. If you're perfect to begin with, just love being with you. **Actually, we're all kind of perfect with all our imperfections but that doesn't mean that we don't need to work on becoming a better person.**

Trust your gut instinct. If you like someone and you know you are going to have a fleeting moment with them and may never see them again but would like to, make a move and invite them to have lunch or dinner with you. Or just ask if they'd like to hang out for a while. Recently, we were on the bus to Tayrona Park near Santa Marta in Colombia and this nice young man started giving us advice about where we were going. A quick conversation established that he was living there with his Colombian wife and they could both give us plenty of up to date information about travelling around the country. I decided to invite them to the boat for dinner. They were a sweet young couple who really enjoyed our hospitality, and we took them for a sail when we returned from our travels around Colombia. Having a local SIM card helps with these sorts of on the spot invitations.

Don't offer to travel with someone too quickly just because you're going in the same direction. You don't want to hook up with someone who is disrespectful of the locals or the environment. I have known people for a few days who have been good company only to see them become obnoxious and loud when they meet up with their friends. One fellow even threw a beer bottle out of the bus window while we were travelling through the countryside after walking the

Inca Trail. I was shocked. I was relieved we were parting ways. So always observe for a short time before you agree to anything and be ready to opt out if you need to. If you've already agreed to, or paid for travel arrangements and then become concerned for your safety, or you're uncomfortable at any time – get out of it. You owe them nothing but an honest exit.

You will find that you will find more interesting and fun people than not. Most people are just wanting to have a good time. I have many friendships now that have grown from hanging out with people for a few days during my travels. Back in 2001 I met a couple on my tour through Europe who have become great friends. They live in the USA and I try to catch up with them every few years. We just clicked and we've had lovely adventures over the years and they've always given me a lovely place to lay my head when I'm in the States. Once we even managed to catch up in Budapest airport for a five minute hug and chat. I was leaving and they were just arriving. It was magical to see them.

Regardless of whether you travel alone or with someone else, the relationships aspect along the way will be paramount to your experience. A companion can make or break a journey and the people you will meet will add to the interesting tales you'll be collecting along the way. While you're away it's important to nurture the relationships back home. If there are changes to be made in those relationships, being away from them is the perfect opportunity to reflect on them and to make decisions about changes that might need to be made within them.

Once you've sorted out your companions, made a choice of your destination or theme it's time to make the plan. This is the detailed layout of what you're setting out to accomplish. It can also be the most onerous parts or one of the most exciting parts of your journey. It depends on your attitude and your approach.

Notes

Plan

Life is what happens when you're busy making other plans.

—John Lennon

ONCE YOU'VE GOT the type of trip you're going to take worked out, then it's time to make a plan. Think of your plan as a blue-print rather than something that is set in concrete. It should just be a skeleton without important details at first.

Knowing everything before you leave home is almost impossible. Travelling is one of those activities that just has to be experienced before you learn the finer details of what's important. You will learn so much more information once you are actually in a country and meeting other travellers who have already been where you're going. This is the best way to get up-to-date information that will influence your choices about destinations and activities.

However, by carrying out smaller journeys before a big one arrives will teach you all sorts of skills, help test out equipment and help with developing an understanding of booking sites and modes of transport.

Brainstorm for all the places that are major destinations for you. It doesn't matter what order you're doing it in because that can be worked out later taking seasons and holidays into consideration. Just get all the destinations down. Once you have this you need to research climate considerations. It's no good booking to go and hike and camp through the Amazon if you pick the wet season. You may want to walk through the forests of Europe picking mushrooms or berries or ski in Whistler. You need to know in which season these activities are possible. If you're adding work into the equation then you need to find out the low and high seasons for whatever you're planning on doing. Once you've investigated these you can get some idea of the direction that will be most viable. If you're buying an 'Around the World' ticket there may be conditions about the direction and the timing of your flights.

The next step is to pinpoint all your destinations on a world map. At this stage don't eliminate anything. You may not be able to do everything you want on your first trip but you don't need to totally discard something either. Some countries have inexpensive flights that might allow you to include a side trip. It is time to research a number of vital facts.

Most countries will require an 'onward ticket' to get into the country and often the airline will check before allowing you to board. So it is important to know your next destination and to have the plans to get there in place. Have the evidence necessary ready to show any boarding or immigration officials. You will need to find out about the requirements of each country as you do your research. During your investigation find out about any visas or travel restrictions that may be in place. Most of this information is on the country's official government website. An 'Around the World' ticket may only qualify if the country is actually listed on the ticket. You may be planning to travel by land through several different countries before you use your plane ticket again so cover your bases and find out what you'll need before you reach the border.

There are many different types of 'Around the World' tickets so you need to find the one that suits your blue-print plan the best. Sometimes a succession of flights that you might find yourself is more flexible and less expensive. It will depend on the succession of places that you're visiting.

When I went on my big year off I booked a very basic round world ticket that took me from Brisbane to L.A., from N.Y. to Frankfurt, from Athens to Bangkok and then back to Brisbane. All my other flights and road trips were organised once I was underway with the exception of some major tours that I already knew that I wanted to do.

I took into consideration the things that I really loved; rainforests, ancient civilisations, spiritualism, volcanoes, waterfalls, hot springs and hiking. I made the decision that I would spend the majority of my money on tours that would incorporate these things. I worked out approximate dates that I would be in a particular location and then I booked a tour that I found on the internet or in a brochure. These dates helped me keep a certain schedule without interfering with other plans. There were some tours, such as visiting the Amazon, that I found less expensive and with more variety when I actually arrived at the destination. Other than booking the first night of accommodation when I would arrive in a new destination, I left my lodgings open so I could move closer to attractions if I wanted to.

Just to reiterate the important details when making your plans, you need to check for major holidays of the country you're visiting, check for visa requirements, ensure you have evidence of ongoing travel, check seasonal restrictions, and book or put aside money for those 'must do' items on your list. I will address each one of these below.

Arriving on a major holiday in a country can cause all types of disruptions to your plans from catching public transport to shopping for your needs. It can also mean that major attractions are crowded and booked out. Pre-carnival in New Orleans meant that the streets were closed at different times for parades. I had planned an excursion into the French Quarter to listen to some bands and I was stranded with no public transport from 5pm until well after midnight. I ended up walking the 5km back to the hostel. I was lucky that I'd gone out with some young gentlemen from the same hostel and had company as I navigated the streets late at night. Another time, after our first overnight crossing on our yacht, Thomas and I discovered that we had lost our propeller. We were travelling from Menorca to Sardinia. We had to be towed in by the coast guard but when we went to arrange a new propeller we found out that August was a holiday month in Italy and we would be lucky to organise anything. You might ask, how can you lose a propeller? Another cruiser joked that it was just the Mafia's way of welcoming us to the country. The point is, it pays to check an official website to get an idea of the country's local and national holidays.

Many countries list their requirements for visas, and the consequences for over staying those visas on their official website. Fortunately, tourists are usually able to stay between 30 – 90 days without filling in any paperwork in most places but you still need to check the requirements for your own nationality. Others require you to fill out an online application that is either free or has a small fee. Make sure you go to the official government websites for these as there are companies that offer you the same form but for a much higher fee. It is often their sites that come up first on an internet search. So check the web address and don't get ripped off. Work visas are a whole different ball game. If you're prepared to do a little bit of work, you will save yourself a lot of money in the long run. Going through an employee agency can be costly and you could be restricted by a contract. Try to organise the visas and the work yourself if you have the time to do the research. The internet is a wonderful world for finding opportunities that will give you the flexibility to work and tour. Give yourself plenty of time in advance for arranging a visa. Some may require you to send your passport away to have the visa entered and some may take quite a few months to arrange. Most will need to be organised before you leave home or from the country where your passport states your nationality. For example if you live in America but you have a New Zealand passport, you will need to apply in New Zealand. It is important to find all the up-to-date information on the official websites of your home country and the country that you plan to visit.

Some countries have quirky rules that have changed the face of travelling in certain regions. Since the introduction of the Schegen Agreement, many foreigners are only allowed to spend a maximum of 90 days out of every 180 days in the whole of the EU region. In the past they could spend up to 90 days in each different country. Many people used to plan a year away travelling through the different countries in Europe but this is no longer an option without risking over-staying your allowance. Fines can result. My advice is to take advantage of the non-EU European countries in amongst the regular haunts.

Evidence of ongoing travel could be a copy of an itinerary or a transportation ticket of some sort. You will have to check and see what the country you are travelling to is willing to accept. Some countries have particular countries identified that they won't accept as a destination as evidence for ongoing travel. A friend of mine arrived at the airport in Australia on his way to the USA with his onward ticket to Mexico to be informed that neither Mexico nor

Canada is accepted as proof that you will be travelling out of the U.S. He quickly had to arrange a flight to another destination in South America before they would allow him onto the plane. This is the sort of information that you don't find out about when you book your tickets online.

The change of seasons in a destination can offer an array of different activities but can also cause certain national parks or attractions to be closed. For example many tours to glaciers are unavailable in the Rockies in Canada in the winter. Many national parks are closed in the USA. during winter also. The Amazon region is flooded for months during the wet season and Greece restaurants and shops practically all shut down over winter. Summer in Europe is crowded, especially during the long school holidays. American countries are similar. Some attractions such as Alcatraz need to be booked days in advance in the summer. For those special places on your list that you really don't want to miss out on, you need to check the seasonal demand.

Seasons influence your job opportunities too. Certain fruits and vegetables have harvesting seasons where pickers are required and the timing may be different in varying regions. Seasons dictate the demand of visitors, therefore opportunities to work in hospitality industries will vary. Research helps determine your work prospects.

Planning your trip and being organised is one of the keys for success but try to leave your options open as you meet new people, hear of fantastic adventures to be had and have a change in your own priorities. Map out your finances to cover your plan and ensure that you don't get caught short.

Notes

Abundance

Every sunrise is priceless and you can experience the richness that life holds only when you live life to the full instead of just being an onlooker.

—Stephen Richards, *Think Your way to Success: Let Your Dreams Run Free*

S PIRITUALISTS HAVE BEEN advocating the law of abundance for a long time now. It goes without saying that there is enough food, money and love in the world for everyone. The problem is with distribution, greed, corrupt politics and natural disasters that seem to determine some people's wealth or lack of it. When I was learning about health, the principal of the college asked me what the hangup was that I had with money. I told him that I didn't have a hangup with money it was just that I didn't like it because the lack of it stopped me from doing things. "Ah ha," he said, "There lies your problem with money." We discussed the use of money as a form of energy and on his advice I read, 'The Little Money Bible,' by Stuart Wilde. It changed my outlook and I have never gone without anything I've needed ever since, and I've felt grateful for everything that I have. That was at least fifteen years ago. It is about the Law of Attraction, service and getting your thoughts straight about cash.

The Law of Attraction is about focusing your energy on a particular target. Attract well-earned, appreciated funds for your up and coming travels by staying positive and well in tune with your purpose for saving. Focus on your target. There are different meditations and activities you can do to bring about a sense of abundance. It includes working, but seeing your work in a positive fulfilling way. For more understanding of the practices involved in this process I have listed some suitable searches in an appendix. I also recommend any of the Self-help gurus: Louise Hay, Deepak Chopra, and Wayne Dyer, just to name a few. They all have a wonderful understanding of this process of creating wealth and explain how to implement it harmoniously within your life. Sometimes when you have a negative attitude towards money it takes a while to shift paradigms. I had read a lot of spiritual books but it wasn't until Stuart Wilde put it so succinctly and lined it up with making money and having a feel for money, did it click. It sounds absurd but I was living the theory of abundance in other areas of my life by being grateful for what I had. I seemed to have deliberately excluded my finances. It almost seemed 'greedy' to tarnish the spiritual realm of my life with money. What I discovered was that it worked in perfect harmony with my self-concept about work and other domains of my life.

Work like you don't need the money

Do what you love. This is the message I instill in my students. Doing what you love to do helps you to enjoy your time at work. It doesn't necessarily mean that you're going to love doing that job for the rest of your life. When I was a teenager I worked in a busy coffee shop along with three of my close friends. We enjoyed excelling in serving the customers efficiently and amused ourselves with lots of practical jokes. We loved rush hour when the time would fly and we would have satisfied many appetites. We would take pride in doing a good job and giving our boss his money's worth with our dedicated labour. I always knew I would do some extra study later on and I went on to complete my high school education at night school before entering university at the age of 22 to become a teacher. It was good for me to do things this way because I had no doubt in the world about what I wanted to do for a career by the time I got there. Sometimes it's best to wait awhile before the inspiration hits you. I was more mature by this time and could concentrate on my studies. This is the beauty of the 'gap' year. Travelling between your time at school and your time in university will hopefully give you the insight required to make choices towards a fulfilling and satisfying career. That way making money will always be a joy.

In the meantime, you might work in conditions less than ideal. But you can always find the positives. You're in charge of the vibe. I hadn't set out to work in a coffee shop but I made the most of it. Whatever you are doing your boss has honoured you by hiring you in the first place. This immediately gives him or her the right to your respect. He or she has respected you enough to trust you. How you are treated after that initial hiring will of course have an impact on how your respect may falter or grow. You can do your best by the relationship by always being cheerful and accommodating, even if you have to fake it some days. I still love the good bosses that I have had the honour of working for both in coffee shops and schools. They are human too and enjoy working with fun-loving people. Having a good attitude makes any work joyful.

When customers are involved, it is also fun to aim to give them a wonderful experience. People are often strapped for time on their lunch breaks so I would do things like memorise regular orders, give the noted customer standing at the back of the crowd a quick silent, 'The Usual?" and on a nod, place their order. By the time they reached the front of the queue I would be handing over their order. They were really appreciative of this service and kept coming back. And that's what work is about. You are offering a service and that service is about making someone's day easier and more fulfilling. Even serving them a cup of coffee. Feel honoured to serve and develop sought after attributes in an employee.

Even if you run your own business in the future, you will understand how good leadership skills and honouring each other, contributes to a happy and productive work environment. Complaining and gossiping are some of the worst attributes your staff could have and you don't need to be a part of it. No matter what sort of job you are doing when you are saving up to travel, always feel grateful that you have this opportunity. Take pride that another human being is trusting you with a task no matter how menial you think it might be. No one in their right mind will judge you when they see that you're working for a higher purpose. And then, love what you do and know that it's the vehicle for new and wonderful adventures.

The greatness of a man is not in how much wealth he acquires,
but in his integrity and his ability to affect those around him positively
— Bob Marley

Notes

Save

There are people who have money and there are people who are rich.

—Coco Chanel

You wouldn't expect your guitar to sound great when not tuned so keep the notes in your bank well-tuned with the vibrations of abundancy.

—Gaylyn

KEEPING A POSITIVE vibe around your money is vital to maintaining a steady flow of inwards funds. There's nothing more disheartening than a huge unexpected bill arriving and eating into your savings for your journey. That's why it's important to set up your bank accounts and your mindset before you even begin. Any money that is put aside for your big trip should become, 'untouchable'. Just cope with what you have without dipping into it. If something unexpected occurs, try to find other avenues to pay for it rather than dipping into your kitty. Try to defer the payment until you can gain extra work or skimp in other areas to pay it off. Once you begin to dip into your travelling budget, it will be hard to stop. So just make it a no-go zone to begin with. This will create a certain vibration that will protect it.

When saving for your trip organise your finances into a couple of different groups. That is what budgeting is all about. Always, always put your money for rent or board at the top. You always want a roof over your head. Keep it inexpensive in a share house or flat if you're not living with your parents or in your own home. Work out how much you need for your journey and put that amount aside before you pay any other bills. Then prioritise your expenses including food, transportation and finally clothing. If you're young, you shouldn't need to put away too much away for health care. Try to use public transport instead of buying a car. You won't have to worry about trying to sell it or finding a place to store it before you leave. There are many ways that you can cut corners to save for your travelling kitty but try to not suffer too many unnecessary hardships to get there.

One of my good friends ate rice and noodles when she was saving for travelling but after staying with me she realised that you can eat great food on a small budget. (See more in my chapter about food). When the exchange rate was particularly bad for Australians going to England, I met a man in London with half a suitcase full of 2 minute noodles. After having lived in England for seven months I could advise him that he could just go to one of the big supermarkets and get delicious pre-made Indian and Chinese meals for a pound. You just had to reheat them in the hostel kitchens. He could have kicked himself. There is no need to go without in the culinary department if you know how to do it. Keep it cheap and healthy. Make use of seasonal fruits and vegetables and always have a variety in your diet. Try some of the recipes out in the chapter about food. You'll probably adjust them to suit yourself and they might even become favourites. They are designed to help you stick within a budget. Another area to make the cuts is on clothing.

Now clothing is an easy one. I usually hand wash my inexpensive items. This way they don't fall apart on the first wash. Second-hand shops offer great items at a low cost. I always choose items that look almost new when shopping in a thrift shop. Other than for work, keep a few basic combinations of tops and bottoms to make up different outfits. This is easier for guys than girls but girls can dress up an item with a few accessories.

Extra items such as birthday and Christmas presents can be a bit lean for the time that you're saving. People will generally understand.

Learn how to do great shoulder massages and foot rubs and make little gift cards for these. Spending quality time with someone can be more important than an inexpensive gift that doesn't really reflect how you feel about a person. If someone asks what you would like for a gift, think of your travels and choose something that you would buy anyway. You don't want extra material possessions if you're going away for a long time but a headlamp or electronic book could make your life more enjoyable.

Once you have saved up enough for your travels make sure you have a 'spending' account if you're travelling for an extended period of time. Set up a weekly sweep of a certain amount that will provide you with your accommodation, travel and food money. If you lose the card connected to that account you won't have too much in there to lose. Have another back up account with a different card that you can access as if it was a credit card. In this account put an amount in to pay for big things like tours or big air fares. Use your first card for transactions on the internet and just sweep over any large amounts needed. Any little excursions should come out of your weekly budget. This way, you'll be able to make decisions about what you can afford for that week. There are so many free adventures to be had and then you can save up over a couple of weeks and have a splurge on something special. **You don't want to waste your money just partying and not be left with money to fly over the Nasca lines or to go paragliding over a canyon. Make your activities count and don't miss out on something special.**

Tip Box

Budgeting Philosophy: Feel rich while you're saving and not spending

List the activities that you do for free –
For example: partake in free exercise programs
Borrow videos from the town library
Borrow your books from the town library
Borrow exercise or yoga videos and carry out your own routines
Surfing, bike riding, skating, visiting a park
Free concerts, displays, museums, carnivals, music jams with friends
Walk to and from work or school
Swap babysitting

Then put a price on all these activities. Make it as much as you like for each. Then note that every time you're doing one of these activities you are saving that much money.

Cooking and Food
Ensure you cook efficiently without using too much energy and avoid wastage by planning your meals ahead of time. Work out how to create new meals with leftovers. Minimise the dishes so it isn't a big chore at the end of the meal to clean up.

Prepare the table nicely using inexpensive candles or place flowers from a tree or garden in the centre. Make it feel special.

Put a price on your meal as if you were eating out. Deduct the estimated amount that you spent on the meal and know that you saved that much money.

Don't nibble while you cook so that it feels as if you didn't even cook the meal when you sit down in front of it. Dress nicely for dinner.

Eat out – I mean outside. Rug up on a winter's night and visit a park with a ready-made hot meal, take dinner down to the lake or the beach, picnic in the backyard or visit a local national park for dinner. Digestion requires you to be at peace with your surroundings. Create your own special corners of the world.

Buy the flights or other transport to a destination in advance so you know you have a limited time to save for the actual trip.

Being a good saver is psychological. You need to feel you're not depriving yourself but maintain a feeling of gratefulness and richness. All this positive action helps you to feel as though you're getting closer to your trip and keeps you feeling optimistic. Avoid retail therapy. Stay away from the shops when you're saving. Do other things with your time. It's not just about the physical side of money. It's about being mindful and enjoying a low-cost lifestyle. (You'll be helping the planet too.)

It pays to have an extra account with some emergency money in it from a different bank than your usual place of business. Card companies have a habit of cancelling **all** of your cards from the same banking institution if you report one stolen. I met a young man in Bogota who had his back pack stolen as he was travelling on an overnight bus. He still had one bankcard left but the card company soon cancelled this one also, despite informing the bank that he would still be using it. This left him and his girlfriend at the mercy of a kind hostel owner who gave them a place to stay while they organised new passports and cards. Money transfers were a problem without his passport for identification too, so always keep a photocopy of your passport in a different place in your luggage. This young fellow was lucky to have found helpful people with resources available to them.

I worked out that $300 was a good amount to have as a weekly budget for my year-long journey in 2012. Maybe add twenty dollars for every year after that that you find yourself reading this. This balanced out between some inexpensive countries like Peru and more expensive countries like USA. I also had strategies such as sailing on yachts in the Mediterranean that cost less per day than a night in a backpackers. All major flights or tours should be paid for before you go. If you need to top this kitty up at any stage you may have to consider working along the way. Before you leave home check your options for your age. Sometimes lining up some employment agencies before you leave will help. You often have to be in your home country to apply for work visas in other countries. **You will definitely need to arrange working visas before leaving home, so be organised months or even a year in advance.**

For a smaller journey, for example between two to five weeks, I always allow $100/day because I'll be trying to fit more action into that shorter time span. I have been doing that for over 30 years and it's still a good rule of thumb.

Tip Box

Budget—Try to stay within these amounts. Some weeks will be more expensive than others. Save up those extra $$$ when you couch surf or stay with friends or relatives to buy tours or to have a night out.

Expense	Daily	Weekly
Accommodation	Average between $10-30	$150-200
Food	$7-$10	$50-$70
Transport and tours	$2-$10	$14-$70
Other		$20

Bonus points: staying with relatives, picking up a free meal, couch surfing, bartering for accommodation and food

Don't wait until you have the best back pack or hiking boots. Buy the basics and get moving. Spending a lot of money at the beginning is telling the Universe the wrong message. I started out with an old suitcase on wheels and found it better than a pack I bought later. You will be able to get what you need along the way. For example; there is no need to carry a tent throughout your travels if you just need it for one part of your trip. There are second hand stores all over the world and other places where you can pick up inexpensive varieties of what you need. I purchased a great ski jacket in a Canadian thrift shop and then gave it away to someone who was travelling to cold places after me. Sometimes people think they can't afford to leave because they have these crazy ideas about buying everything before they go. Trust me. You won't have room to pack everything before you go. **Try to use what you have already and get going. On the way, you learn to go without and you become grateful for the lighter load.**

Notes

Bargains

Money is only a tool. It will take you wherever you wish, but it will not replace you as the driver.

—Ayn Rand

PATIENCE AND ENERGY are required to save on expenditure. When entering negotiations always be clear which currency you are dealing in and be aware of the local customs involved. A common thing to be aware of is that a trader has change in a currency that you can use. Some of the visitors to our boat in the Caribbean bartered for a sun lounge for a day on the beach and felt happy with their bargaining skills until, their change arrived in the form of two mangoes and a coconut. They could afford to laugh it off as an experience and their change was delicious. However, some traders count on you being in a hurry and run off to get change from one of their colleagues or try to get you to take something else from their shop instead. Sometimes this is harmless and you can pick up some small souvenirs that you can give away as presents but other times you might be counting on those funds.

It is wise to know about gem scams or 'custom-made' jewellery for the local area you are dealing in. Buying anything of great value should be treated with great caution. There aren't usually many real bargains on these items and unless you're an expert in this field, you may be easily deceived.

It will often take a little bit of research once you arrive at a destination to make the most of the local deals. It is best not to book activities as soon as you arrive so you have an opportunity to scope out the deals and variety of tours on offer. Talk to others at the hostel to see if they have done a similar trip. Depending on the day you arrive or the length of your stay, you should try to have an orientation day at first. This allows you to gauge what you want to do and find out what you can do on your own or if you need to pay a guide. Take in the sights and roam about. If there are any special activities pertinent to that area, you will find many scouts or offers at booths bargaining for your coin.

One place we wanted to visit was the salt cathedral in a small village just north of Bogota, Zipaquirá. In the streets we were approached by hawkers selling tours for what seemed a reasonable price, but when we looked at the public transport system and asked for advice at the hostel, we found that we could get there ourselves for a tenth of the cost of one ticket. It ended up being extremely easy and enjoyable doing it at our own pace.

Another place full of deals and options are the Galapagos Islands. Any island that you land on will have deals and options for tours for visiting the other islands. You don't need to take the face value. Feel free to negotiate for a more personalised tour and for a price that you're willing to part with.

Once again be on the lookout for scam tour operators who just want to get you to shops for a commission of their sales. This can easily happen in places like Thailand where a tuk tuk driver can waste your precious day away.

You may also need to consider the local customs on tipping tour operators. Even though you've parted with a substantial amount, they still may want a percentage in tips.

Sometimes an activity such as caving, surfing, bungee jumping, rafting or other extreme sports, may be much less expensive than in your home country. Places like Colombia have a few destinations like this where thrill seekers can experience all the previously mentioned activities plus mountain bike riding, paragliding or horse riding at a fraction of what it costs in Australia, New Zealand or U.S.A., and the scenery is spectacular. Of course you have to decide if the workplace health and safety regulations are up to your standards, but in most places you will find they are. Make sure your travel insurance covers you for involvement in such activities. Skiing and even motorbike riding cover can incur extra costs. This might be a great opportunity for trying something new that you would normally be unable to afford.

When we were in San Gil in Colombia, where many sports are available, we met a young Irish girl. She had a few stitches on her face and some massive bruises that were turning yellow. After some polite small talk I got up the courage to ask her which of the dangerous activities on offer had she collected her bodily souvenirs. She laughed and informed us that she'd tripped over on the pavement and hit her head. Unperturbed after a night in hospital, she went on to go paragliding the next day. It just goes to show that a few bruises can always be thrown in with the bargain if you're not careful.

Set your budget and stay within it. As long as I have clean sheets, can lie flat and can lock up my valuables, I can have a good night's sleep. Most hostels will make up your bed for you but if they don't it's a good idea to make your bed when you arrive and before you head off for a night out. You don't want to wake anyone later on if you come in late, and a properly made bed will help you to feel comfortable for a good night's sleep. This is one of the most valuable things you can have. Try not to spend too much money on accommodation. There are other options other than staying in hostels such as Couch Surfing or travelling on yachts. I prefer to pay my own way so I have my independence and I'm not stuck in the suburbs somewhere on someone's couch, but some people have developed wonderful friendships from this experience. Others I've met have been given the full local tour and have been well integrated into the family. Each experience will be different. It's a personal choice on what you'd prefer to do and the best way would be to mix it up a little bit. Hostels tend to be on major bus routes or in the centre of town so can save a lot of trouble and money with getting around a strange city. It's a good idea to check the distance between your arrival place and your hostel and have an idea of how much to spend if you need to resort to hiring a taxi.

I have made lots of friends during my travels around the world and it is a lot of fun visiting them and having them coming to visit me. They're usually interesting people and interesting people usually choose somewhere interesting to live. It's a win-win situation. It's always nice to catch up with family members too if they're along the path. They are usually happy to offer a room for the night which can save a lot of money in the end. Once I remember waking up in my cousin's house in Florida. I looked around at the nice surroundings but had forgotten where I was. Realising I was alone, I thought, "What the hell? I can't afford a private room." I was relieved when I remembered where I was. Relatives and friends always know that the hospitality is reciprocal.

Staying in hostels is a great way not to waste money unnecessarily on your journey. Accommodation can take up more than the best of your budget if you are not willing to utilise this world-wide resource. Not only are you likely to be staying in a unique building, but you are also creating a unique experience for yourself by staying in hostels. Immediately, the benefit of the cost is prominent. Being able to cook your own meals allows you to save a lot of money although not all hostels have a kitchen. You need to check before you arrive somewhere. But the most amazing advantage is the different locations that are available.

All over the world you will find a hostel where no other accommodation is affordable on the budget I mention. If you are staying in a big city, find a central hostel and save transport costs and time getting around. There are often discounts available for local attractions and you will meet others who might want to join up to share the costs of car hire or to make up the numbers for a tour. Most of all you will have the opportunity to meet other travellers from all corners of the planet.

Don't forget to consider joining a yacht for part of your travel, assisting families in destinations in return for accommodation and share rides. Website addresses are listed in the appendix.

The important message that you're sending the Universe when you're hunting for bargains is to do it as a means to conserve resources – avoiding waste, not being extravagant and doing it out of choice and not necessity. As soon as necessity enters the equation there is a feeling of desperation and neediness. Fear can creep in and work against you. Always keep your kitty topped up while you're enjoying the challenges of a good bargain hunt. In return, you will find that when you apply the Law of Attraction, your needs will be met.

Tip Box

Bargain Hunting at Home and Beyond

- Buy clothes on sale, from garage sales or from second hand clothing shops.
- Shop late in the afternoon when prices are dropped on items from the bakery or meat department.
- Purchase dips and cheeses when they're on sale and freeze them for when you have visitors.
- Buy generic items instead of known brands.
- Only buy what you love to eat or love to wear.
- Look for particular days for cheap flights.
- Look for cheap movie theatres and go on the cheaper nights.
- Spoil yourself every now and then with something special but inexpensive.
- Learn how to give and receive massages.
- Find different travel options that are either free or very inexpensive.
- Have a skill such as tarot card reading on hand to barter with.

Notes

Pack

He who would travel happily must travel light.

—Antoine de Saint-Exupéry

MOST EXAMPLES FOUND in books or on the internet of suggested packing lists will be stressing about packing light and this is so true. It is also important to take clothes that will feel good, look good and dry quickly. The girl's list is slightly different because of course we're made differently and have different needs. I saw one packing list that said you only need three pairs of undies maximum. That was obviously a list for boys not girls. That's one thing us girls can afford to be fussy about as our undies are small and don't take up much room any way. Girls might also want to invest in taking a supply of their regular sanitation products for the time they're away. Not all products are available in every country.

When choosing items, remember that most things should be able to dry overnight so don't pack many clothes made from thick heavy materials. If you're travelling in cold countries, pack layers of shirts made from light material.

Only buy a backpack if you plan to actually hike a long way through a jungle, even a concrete jungle. A suitcase on robust wheels has better accessibility and it doesn't tire your back as much. A good option is to purchase a big wheeled suitcase that has the straps to carry on your back. This is great if you have to carry it over rough roads. We have one of these and it's fantastic. It also pays to have at least two small netted bags where small clothing items can be stored and easily accessible. Chargers and electrical items can be stored in a small drawstring nylon bag. This helps to keep track of these important items and makes them ready to grab in an instant. I can't tell you how many times I've seen people run around their dorm late at night looking for their chargers.

If you're purchasing a backpack you will want it to be super light. Try to choose one with a zipper that opens all the way around so you can access your gear without having to dig everything out. Ensure it is the right size for your body. Compartments are good to separate shoes, toiletries, dirty washing and electrical gear. Seek expert advice.

Compartmentalise everything. Have specific items in soft drawstring bags. A dry bag is important for electronics. Try a 'Pelican' bag if your main bag is big enough. Use cloud storage or good quality memory sticks for photos and movies. Having all your belongings sorted and easily accessible takes a lot of the stress out of packing and repacking away.

Keep it light. Around 10-15kg will keep you within acceptable weights for budget airlines, although you may need to purchase extra luggage allowance at the time of booking.

Standard Needs For Everyone

- Small pair of scissors.
- A roll of duct tape.
- Nail clippers.
- A small lock with the key on a lanyard.
- A small pencil case with a simple can opener, knife, fork and spoon.
- Toiletries—shampoo, a soap container, toothbrush, hair brush, toothpaste, face cloth, shaving gear, any other special needs. (Keep this small as they can take up a lot of space.)

- Sarong—great to wear to the bathroom so you don't leave any items behind or to wear around your head for protection from the sun.
- Small towel.
- Clothing—1 quick dry shorts and 1 long pants (dark colours dress up a bit but can also be hot when hiking—choice is yours), 1 suitable sun shirt, 1 sweatshirt (if you need more buy a souvenir one along the way), 1 small waterproof jacket. (If going to a cold climate, 1 dress jacket that can double up as a blanket), 3 t-shirts, 2 shorts or skirts, 1 dress shirt, maybe a pair of jeans although these can be heavy if you're a big guy, at least four pairs of underwear, swimming costume.
- Hat.
- Small bottle of sun protection, lip balm, sun glasses, cap.
- Water bottle—the collapsible kind.
- Pen and notebook. (Journal plus a book to write all your bookings down in and any shopping lists.)
- A set of social cards with your photo and contact details to hand out.
- A packet of plastic zip lock bags.
- A marker pen to mark your food in hostels.
- Passport in a waterproof bag.
- Camera and charger.
- Phone and charger.
- Music player and charger.
- A universal power adapter.
- Small cloth bag for groceries. (Buy a souvenir one along the way.)

Extra Girl's Stuff

- A warm long wide scarf but made of light material. (Use as a skirt, blanket or as an accessory to dress up plain clothes.)
- A nice dress for going out and a small pair of dress up sandals to match.

- A small amount of makeup—you won't wear this often so just the basics.
- Little extras that help you feel as though you can dress up and feel good—a hair straightener if that's what it takes.
- I took a nice plastic wine glass because I wanted something nice to drink out of. You can't always find something nice in a hostel and this is where I would do most of my socialising.

Rehearse your packing by going on a weekend away with what you have. Practise keeping it tidy and washing items as you go. If you're using a backpack and plan on doing some serious hiking then it's a good idea to do a bit of training with your backpack before you go. You will quickly learn your limitations and comfort requirements. Remaining light, having comfort and ease of keeping clean are the three main goals of selecting clothing and items to pack. 'Keep it simple' is a great motto to have. Remember, you can always purchase something later if you find you're missing something.

Notes

Essentials

YOUR TRAVEL IS about you having a wonderful time while learning about others and yourself so you want things to go smoothly. Active planning in being as self-sufficient as possible when travelling is the beginning of keeping the vibe in a positive motion. Here are just a few tips that have unfolded along my journey about passports, insurances, health, visas and watching out for the 'fine print.'

It goes without saying that your passport is your most important document to safeguard while travelling abroad. Most countries require you to have at least six months remaining before it is due to expire – after the date that you're meant to leave their borders. This is in case there are any mishaps that may delay your departure. So if you're travelling for a long period of time, you may need to renew your passport while you're away. This can be done at most consulates of your country. It's a good idea to purchase a small waterproof pouch for your passport before you leave home. Always have your passport in your luggage that you keep with you during bus or train trips. Keep a photo copy of the main page in a different part of your luggage. Lock it away with your luggage when you're at a hostel or keep it in a safe. Life can become very difficult if you lose it. Should this happen, contact your consulate immediately.

Health and travel insurance is a must for long or short term travel. You never know when you might need it. I tend to have it to cover me for the 'big' things – helicopter rescue and lots of hospital cover. Little things can usually wait until you get home or won't break the bank by having them seen to overseas. Some countries have free medical for everyone, including visitors, and dental care can be less expensive in some countries. My travel agent negotiated with a couple of travel insurance companies for me and within ten minutes had an offer of half the original price from the same reputable company. I saved nearly one thousand dollars and paid nine hundred dollars for the year and that included ski cover. So shop around and get an expert to help you. If you're travelling with someone, make sure that they are considered to be your travelling partner on the policy and are included in any return flights or accommodation in case of an emergency. Be proactive in maintaining your health by taking care of your diet and of hygiene.

Keeping yourself and your belongings clean helps to maintain your wellbeing. The sniff test doesn't count when you're doing it yourself on yourself. Make the most of showers when they're available. Wear as little as possible to a communal shower to avoid losing belongings. A sarong works well. Take all your toiletries in one bag. Clip any watches or valuables onto your bag so you don't leave them behind. Getting your laundry done can be time consuming and a pain. Some hostels will have a laundry service but quite often they are expensive. Hostels where machines are available to the guests are often in use for the bedding in the mornings so the evenings are the best time to try and use them. You can avoid all this if you wash out your clothes in the showers when you are washing yourself. Give them a good wringing out and hang them around your bed. This is good to do if you have another day of staying there. This way your laundry never becomes an issue. Don't leave wet smelly clothes in your pack. Have a few plastic bags on hand to pack away damp or wet items then get them out of your bag as soon as possible. Having a system in place for getting your laundry done will give you spare time to rest up when you're feeling a bit exhausted.

Having a rest day is an important part of keeping healthy. If you overdo it with too much action on some days, have down time with a good book or good company. Pace yourself by including relaxation into the journey. Aim for days lazing on beaches or a swim in a rock pool where you can spend a few hours at least. Although you will be doing a lot of running around sightseeing, try to include some yoga and relaxation exercises in amongst it all. Maintaining a calm mind and a relaxed persona are vital for your health and well-being. Eat well and don't over indulge in food or drink. I have lots of information about healthy eating in the chapter about food and I have given a brief outline of my health philosophy at the back of the book.

Being prepared with any official documentation will assist you to remain relaxed. Most countries have good internet sites that will notify you of the need of any visas for your nationality. A good travel agent will do the same. There are some tricky little rules that aren't obvious that can complicate things if you're unaware of them.

As mentioned in another chapter, at the time of writing this an onward ticket from the United States to either Canada or Mexico didn't cover the requirements of an onward ticket and many unwary travellers had to purchase extra flights at the last minute to be able to get into the country. This means that if you are flying into the USA, and you only have a ticket from there to either Mexico or Canada, they won't let you leave your home country. They won't let you on the plane without a ticket to a different country. What may seem to be obviously a different country to us, doesn't constitute as one in this case. So make sure you have a ticket to another country other than those two or a return ticket home.

There are other tricky ins and outs for non-Europeans now that the Schengen Agreement is in. People from most other nations used to be able to travel in each European country for up to ninety days. At the time of writing this, it is now ninety days **in total** for all EU countries combined. This doesn't leave enough time if you were hoping to tour for a year. Some countries aren't included in this count and that's where it becomes tricky to work out if you're illegally overstaying or not. New Zealand passport holders could stay 180 days in comparison to most other nationalities. But they are still limited to 90 days in one country. Do your research and seek expert advice with your particular travel itinerary. The consulate of your own country will be able to assist you.

Don't count on the hearsay from this book or any other source other than the official websites or brochures from the countries concerned. Details change all the time for some countries and are dependent on the political climate.

Speaking of climates, if you want to remain travelling light but you think you might need special equipment along the way to suit a variety of temperatures, begin with a list of the minimum requirements. Keeping your shopping list for major items brief will assist you in carrying cumbersome items along the way. If you can avoid buying, particularly if you are unlikely to use it again, then all the better. Try to take advantage of second-hand shops for large coats or ski gear. You don't need the very best tent to camp for a short time if you're going in good weather or your own climbing or dive gear. Research any specialist equipment you might need and find out if there are clubs or organisations nearby that you can join as a temporary member. They will usually welcome a visitor to join them for a while and someone there might be happy to loan you the gear or you could organise to hire it. That's certainly normal for dive and climbing gear but some people prefer to buy their own. You have to work out if it is really worth it to carry it with you or not. Avoid complications at airports by ensuring you don't exceed your luggage allowance when you purchase extra items. Some airlines get a little bit precious with their rules and it pays to read the fine print.

We're all guilty of clicking the 'I agree to the terms and conditions' box without really reading the fine print but sometimes it is certainly worthwhile to skim those pages and to work out the finer details. Before you launch off on an economy airline flight you need to have a good understanding of what is included and I highly recommend that you read the terms and conditions. Many of them fly in and out of obscure airports a long way from major centres inspite of calling that airport a similar name to the main one. From Frankfurt I was to fly to Finland with one such airline. I arrived early at the main airport to find out that particular airline actually flew from an airport 135km away but used 'Frankfurt' in front of the actual name of the airport. My air ticket hadn't been that cheap so I didn't want to lose it. I quickly found out how to get a bus there and I made it in plenty of time. Upon arrival I found out that my backpack was one kg over the allowance and it was going to cost 20 Euro to have it on board so I unpacked approximately 1kg of items into my carry-on luggage. While I was standing in line I saw two young guys who'd obviously not read the fine print about having to print off your own boarding pass or it would be a fee of 50, yes, 50 Euro, handing over their hard earned cash. In the meantime I lined up to get on the plane and discovered at the gate that my small fat backpack would now not fit into the frame of the carry-on luggage checker. Oh, that will be 50 Euro thanks. No thank you. I left the line with 45 minutes still to board the plane and purchased a bag for 20 Euro and made it fit. I wished I'd just paid the original 20 Euro for my luggage. It was a very confusing and complex process which I would recommend you aim to avoid.

Some situations really warrant reading the fine print. Insurance, visa requirements, contracts of employment or purchasing a property, websites, to know if you're handing over all the rights to the material you're placing on there... the list goes on. It's almost a conspiracy to make these terms and conditions as boring as possible so you don't read them thoroughly. I think they should include cartoons or text box hints on the really important stuff. These sort of things complicate a simple life, so keep it in mind to spend some time on these matters.

Notes

Sleep

As long as I can lie flat, the sheets are clean, my bags are safe and there's minimal snoring – I can sleep.

—Gaylyn

Sleep is that golden chain that ties health and our bodies together

—Thomas Dekker

HAVING A GOOD night's sleep is vital for a clear mind and healthy body. You need to feel safe and comfortable. I have added this chapter with a brief synopsis of places to stay to provide an overview to help you make decisions about how you might diversify your approach to accommodation. Each type of budget or free accommodation has its pros and cons and you have to decide what suits you. I have listed some of these but your personal preferences will determine whether they're an option for you. I have also listed some booking websites that I have personally used and found suitable in the appendix.

I would normally have at least four or five pages open on the web when I book accommodation. One page will be about the main tour I want to do in that area, checking for availability on the dates I want to go. One will be a Google Map showing me where that attraction

is located. One will be the hostel
booking page. Another will
be a map showing me
the distance from the
hostel I am looking at
to the attraction. The
final page will be about
transport either locally

or actually getting to the city or town. I will
use all these pages to coordinate timing and
positioning to minimise travel costs and to make the most of my time
in the location. This strategy becomes quick the more practice you
have with it.

Hostels — These are my first choice, especially when they are
aligned with Hostels International as you can expect a high standard
of cleanliness and bed comfort.

Pros	Cons
- Usually fantastic old buildings with unique themes such as old sailing ships, jails, castles, windmills, heritage mansions. - Great for company if you're travelling alone. - A variety of rooms are often on offer. - Costs aimed at budget travellers. - Good advice on what's on in town. - Language lessons are often available. - Kitchens are usually well equipped. - Get to meet lots of other travellers in the common room and kitchen. - Usually close to attractions. - Usually on main transport routes. - Multi-lingual staff usually available. - Book swaps. - Movies often available. - Board games often available. - Social gatherings and jam sessions often occur. - Lockers are usually available. - Laundry services often available at a reasonable price. - Often close to the centre of town. - Breakfast often on offer. - No need to carry bedding or camping gear. - Usually close to nightlife or have specials at their in-house bars.	- Sometimes no choice of dorm buddies. - Can be noisy. - Can be a bit dusty. - Quality of bathrooms can vary. - Other guests can be a bit thoughtless. - Kitchen can be unkempt. - You're sharing with others.

Budget hotels are the least favourite of mine but sometimes you need to be close to an airport and then this becomes a good option.

Pros	Cons
- Privacy — good if you need a break from people. - Usually quiet. - Clean. - Inexpensive. - Entertainment usually available.	- Can be noisy. - Poor quality fittings. - Can be in obscure or sleazy locations.

Luxury hotels are more of a favourite of mine but I actually prefer hostels for the experiences that I have there. I added this in in case your idea of a budget was different to mine.

Pros	Cons
- Nice fittings and furnishings. - Great service. - Nice restaurants. - Entertainment availability. - Luxurious	- Expensive. - Can be a bit lonely.

Couch surfing is something I haven't done but I've encountered lots of people who have.

Pros	Cons
- You get to meet a local with insider information. - You can make new and wonderful friends. - You are shown the sights. - It's usually free. - They will often pick you up. - You could end up in wonderful surroundings.	- You could end up in the suburbs away from everything. - You might not get along with your host or you find the place distasteful. - You don't know what you're getting into.

Sailing on vessels that you connect with through internet sites.

Pros	Cons
- Travel as you stay. - Adventurous. - Learn new skills. - Meet wonderful people. - Inexpensive or free. - Exciting. - Open air experience. - Visit many different countries. - Learn to be versatile. - Meet amazing people. - See amazing sunsets and places. - Relaxing.	- Don't even think of it if you get seasick. - Can be cramped. - May have a lack of privacy. - Can be trapped with someone you don't know. - You will only have a small space to yourself. - Can be a slow way to travel. - Limited water. - Challenging cooking conditions. - May get a bit scary. - Boat may not be well maintained.

Home/farm stays, house sitting, running hospitality businesses, camping and volunteering are all other options that provide accommodation. They too will have their pros and cons. Variety is the spice of life. Mix it up a little and try it all. Accommodation costs can eat up your budget. Every time you have a night's stay that is free, you can tick that off as a huge saving. Friends of mine have travelled for three years and have only spent money on less than a week's accommodation in that whole time. They have used a combination of staying with family, staying and working with a host family, camping and sailing. This has enabled them to spend money on other activities. So it is possible and I hope they write a book to share their strategies.

Sleep is the best meditation

—Dalai Lama

Notes

Eat

If more of us valued food and cheer and song above hoarded gold, it would be a merrier world.

—J.R.R. Tolkien

BREAKING BREAD WITH each other brings about conversation and laughter. Never has a medium helped to make so many joyous memories. Even eating in quiet solitude with a beautiful view can bring about a contented relaxed feeling. If you're serious about saving money on food, get yourself a tiny little cooler bag and freeze and refreeze a bottle of water to keep things cool and take some tomatoes, cheese, boiled egg, peanut butter and crackers to have for lunch along the way or out on an excursion. This has saved me from going hungry numerous times when I've happened to arrive on a public holiday that I didn't know about or nothing suitable is available that was value for money. Add a cloth shopping bag that can be folded away when not in use to carry your crackers and any dry goods that you may decide to carry to the next destination. I also take a small pencil case with a sharp knife, a fork and a spoon. I have a handy little army can opener, a vegetable peeler and a miniature grater too. Check out the army disposal stores for purchasing any special items.

My food basics that I carry with me are, crackers, stock cubes, soya sauce, peanut butter and

KITCHEN

127

a small bag of flour (don't try to get on a plane with the bag of flour in a country renowned for cocaine production), and a small bottle of cooking oil – look for one with a good lid, (Nutella for crepes and a treat). Everything else I leave behind at hostels for others to use. There isn't usually much left but that's okay. You might go out to eat one night and not get to use some of the ingredients that you've bought. Note: take a black permanent marker to label your bags of shopping as per required by the hostel.

Living in a world that has extremes from waste to poverty in all sorts of forms, it is nice to know that a helpful traveller is doing their bit by leaving a bit of food behind at the hostels that wasn't suitable to be flown out or worth carrying away. Rather than throwing it in the rubbish bin it can be put to good use. Keep the good karma happening by leaving your excess food in an accessible place for others to utilise. This includes bread, rice, noodles, cans or packets of anything you don't want to carry with you. It will be appreciated and the favour will be returned. (That doesn't mean leaving behind your mouldy leftovers in the fridge though).

So, before you go out shopping when you arrive at a place, check the free shelf and reassign what you will be able to use. Always check the use by dates and if any creepy crawlies have had the opportunity to invade the contents. I've never experienced this while travelling, only in my pantry at home in Australia.

Make the most of what you find. We were snowed in at Jasper and the weekend skiers had left bread rolls, pasta sauce, cheese in the fridge, a pancake mix, rice and various other things. My travel buddy and I had a few meals combined with our own vegetables and I made pizzas and pancakes for everyone who was around at the time. It made for a warm, sharing atmosphere around the huge fireplace.

Eating out can be fun, cheap and/or expensive but cooking for yourself saves lots of money and you get what you want. It can be a lot of fun cooking all together in a big kitchen. You might have to scramble around for a good saucepan and fry pan and wash up as you go but it is well worth it to know what is in your food.

Tip Box

Ten Great Ways to use Flat Breads

1   As a wrap with peanut butter, boiled egg slices, salad and a touch of sweet chilli sauce, (or whatever you love).
2   Pizza base.
3   Samosa pastry—cut into quarters, place left over curry inside, set fingers and squeeze sides together and fry in a little bit of oil. Yummy with a bit of sweet chilli sauce.
4   Dipping bread—cut into eighths, use a paper towel to wipe on some oil, add some herbs and lightly fry in some oil or cook without herbs to use as a side dish for a curry.
5   As a Burrito with Mexican beans and salad.
6   Lasagne sheets.
7   Egg in the hole—fold into quarters and pull a small circle out from the middle about the size of an egg yolk, squeeze some cheese in between the flaps, place in a frypan at a very low heat, break the egg into the hole, sprinkle a bit more cheese on top and the pieces of leftover bread from the hole you made. Cover with a lid. It won't take long but it needs to be on a low heat or the bottom of the egg will burn and that's not nice.
8   As a taco shell—fold in half and fry lightly each side before filling.
9   Garlic bread—similar to the dipping bread but add crushed garlic.
10 As a pastry base for a quiche or other pie.

Luckily many hostels are set up close to supermarkets so you won't have to carry your things too far. You don't want to buy too much either. Work out a menu for the next three or so days, depending on how long you're staying in one spot and only buy the things required with a few treats thrown in. Some hostels include a simple breakfast but you can still add to that if needed. There are little tricks to avoid food wastage that I will share here. Of course don't include anything you don't like and the availability will be affected by the country through which you are travelling. The following is usually good for the Caribbean, South America, Europe, United States of America, Australia, New Zealand and most Asian countries. If you are having difficulty getting anything, leave it out, substitute or go and eat some local foods and ask where to buy anything you like. I have had to be very creative on some Caribbean islands.

First 2/3 Day Shopping List

500g rice, a dozen eggs, a small bottle of soy sauce, (check the free shelf first), a packet of stock cubes — the smallest you can find, a small bottle of vegetable oil, can of coconut milk, box of milk, cheap packet of spaghetti or two minute noodles, a small 500g bag of flour, crackers, a box of cereal, curry powder although many herbs and sauces can usually be found on the free shelves.

Fresh produce: Fruit for breakfast and snacks, 3 tomatoes, 1 head of broccoli, 3 large carrots, green or red peppers/capsicum and half a cauliflower, 2 potatoes, 1 sweet potato, 3 onions, small piece of ginger, any meat you might want to throw in. I'm vegetarian and it makes cooking a lot easier.

3 day Menu with the Above Shopping List
—recipes are in the appendix

➢ Fruit and cereal for breakfast each day.
➢ Lunches of snacks and crackers.

➤ Dinners (recipes in appendix): 1. curried vegetables and rice. 2. crepes and leftover curry. 3. stir fried vegetables with noodles.

➤ Left overs – make a frittata, fried rice with left over rice to take on the road, boiled eggs, pancakes or scrambled eggs for breakfast.

Second Shopping List, Maybe in a New Location

A packet of tortillas or similar flat bread, can of red kidney beans, taco flavouring mix, packet of grated cheese, can of hotdogs or vegetarian hotdogs, small can of tuna or fresh mushrooms, can of peeled tomatoes/cream, a tub of plain yoghurt, packet soups if in cold climate

Fresh produce: a small packet of mushrooms, small lettuce, carrot, small avocado, 3 onions, peppers, fruit, 1 lime or lemon

Menu with the Second Shopping List

➤ Breakfasts as above.

➤ Lunch: try local food or as above.

➤ Dinners (quick easy recipes below): tuna or mushroom pasta with salad, pizza with salad, tortillas  with beans.

➤ Left overs: make salad wraps with peanut butter and chilli sauce for lunches. Add a piece of chicken, egg or cold meat if you desire.

You will discover your favourites and make personal adaptations to the above meals. You will be surprised how much variety there is in these small lists of food.

Even if you consider your time cooking to be social time, you don't want to be spending all of your time in the kitchen, so I have included recipes in the appendix that take about half an hour including chopping up. You don't want to hog the kitchen space either. Make sure you wash up as you go. Just your pots and pans should be left to soak until you've finished your meal. Share the load and invite others to join you.

Store any leftovers for use the next day in a clean container with a lid. Place your name and date on it and store in the communal refrigerator. I actually hide my leftovers in my grocery bag in the fridge. Once I caught a hungry not-quite-sober guy munching away at my leftovers. At least he enjoyed them but it mucked up my menu for the next day.

Tip Box

Great things to do with leftovers—they make a great quick meal

- Fry up left-overs and add a scrambled egg over the top. Cook and flip. Add a bit of cheese.
- Use left-over fried rice to put inside a vegetable such as a pepper/capsicum with the centre taken out. Bake in a fry pan with a bit of oil and the lid on so the vegetable cooks through.
- Use left-over mince or bean mix to fill in a baked potato. Add cheese and melt.
- Mix left-over noodles with mayonnaise and mustard to make an interesting cold salad. Add a bit of finely diced onion and a can of corn.
- Put any left-over curry on hot toast.

Invite others early on to share. Ingredients like rice and pasta make a meal go further. It won't cost you much to invite someone to share your meal. Make some extra crepes and have Nutella and strawberries for dessert. Invite them to join in on the process and cleaning up as well. Hostels can be quiet around dinner time depending on the availability of inexpensive eateries nearby. Strike up a conversation and find a new friend early and invite them to share your meal with you.

The Indian Feast

When you meet a few people who don't mind cooking, suggest that each one of them brings a small curry to the table. Along with the different curries have some of these sides. Fried eggplant with thinly sliced rings of onion and chilli in coconut milk, banana and coconut in yoghurt or coconut milk, thin slices of cucumber with tiny dices of onion and garlic covered in yoghurt, sour cream or coconut milk, fried plantains, flat bread cut into 8 wedges and lightly fried in oil, a bowl of tiny diced tomato/onion/coriander/garlic/cucumber with lemon juice squeezed on it. This makes for a hearty delicious feast that will keep people chatting for ages. Enjoy.

Yummy Sides and Extras

Diced chips—dice some potatoes and put in 2 teaspoonfuls of oil, put a lid on and cook at a medium heat. Sprinkle a stock cube over them and let them cook a bit more. Turn over regularly. Cook until slightly browned.

Marinated tofu and peanut sauce—marinate tofu in a mixture of 1 teaspoonful of honey or sugar, 30 mL of soya sauce, chilli, onions diced very small, $1/2$ cup of water or juice. Slice the tofu thinly for burgers and in cubes for a stir fry. Marinate for a few hours or over night. Peanut sauce—use marinade from tofu and put in a small saucepan at a low heat. Cook for 2 minutes. Add a big heaped spoonful of peanut butter. Stir for 2 more minutes.

Greek salad, (my way)—A mixture of green leafed vegetables shredded, small tomatoes, olives, feta and cucumber diced. Mix together and add a dressing of oil, garlic and herbs. Great with pastas.

Carrot and coconut salad—grate some carrot and add dried coconut, sultanas and sprinkle some lime juice and honey over it.

Vietnamese Summer Rolls—Buy some inexpensive rice paper sheets and string rice noodles. Lightly boil string rice noodles and then remove from saucepan, Use warm water to briefly soak rice paper sheets one at a time. Place two dessert spoons of ingredients such as cucumber, carrot, fried omelette, lettuce to the rice noodles and place in the bottom quarter of the round rice paper sheets. Roll like in an envelope. This is a great one to have everyone make their own.

Tip Box

Garlic Butter

The key to great garlic bread is to mix the garlic into the butter really well. Get your friend to stir it for about 3 minutes while you get the bread ready.

Nutrition

Try to eat as much raw food as possible. This takes up less energy when digesting it. All the above recipes are ones I use when I feel like creature comforts and sharing my food. I have tried to stay conventional also because my health philosophy is quite specialised. I try to have as many salads and as much fruit as possible. A good variety of these are available in most local markets. Try to have a variety of proteins such as avocado, nuts and dried fruits, egg or cheese. You don't need a lot but you do need three different kinds during one day to stay healthy. I don't usually have breakfast either as the body is still detoxing in the morning. Chew your food well and if you're not hungry—don't eat. I often skip meals when I'm travelling and this helps to keep me fit and well. It gives your digestion a rest and you're not over taxing it. I would rather go without than eat some junk food being sold at a truck stop. Mainly, I pack a healthy salad wrap and some fruit when I'm on the road. If you are interested in reading more about my health philosophy I suggest you read what I've written in the the back of the book and research some websites.

Fresh Water

Make sure you have fresh pure water all the time during your travels. Unfortunately, this often means purchasing it and plastic bottles are a world problem. Try and buy a large bottle and refill a small one along the way if you don't have your own.

Eating is a part of the cultural experience of any place that you visit and you should always try some of the local cuisine. However, it is always nice to have some of the creature comforts of home by making some of your favourite dishes. Some countries have inexpensive eateries and others are so expensive that eating out can become inhibitive as it will literally eat away at your funds. Find a balance and ensure you eat plenty of fresh fruit along the way.

Notes

Risks

Don't be too timid and squeamish about your actions. All life is an experiment. The more experiments you make the better.

—Ralph Waldo Emerson

THE BIGGEST RISK of all is not to live life to the fullest, but of course we need to be realistic. No matter how many guardian angels are watching over you there are real dangers out there in this big world. Ignoring these would only mean to live in a day dream of false security. As our experiences are about adapting to this physical world, these dangers need to be taken into consideration. However, by worrying about them and fearing things that 'might' happen, you will attract them towards you. Just like attracting the good things, we can attract the bad as well. The result will depend on whereever your energy is focused. So take some precautions, count on your intuition and don't put yourself in any deliberate danger.

It is continually the case of picking up on the vibe and avoiding certain people and places. Remember the conscious point of decision making, recognise the vibe and act accordingly.

You can actively alter the vibe by carrying out different thought processes. I protect myself by white lighting any vehicle I am travelling in or any place where I am staying. You can do this by imagining a square based pyramid of shining white light with an inverted matching pyramid on the bottom of it. I make each wall of the shape by beginning at the apex and connecting it altogether by imagining the light. I build the protection around me. I have had amazing experiences having done this and I continue to white light our yacht on almost a daily basis. I know I am as safe as I can possibly be and it gives me great confidence to tackle the high seas.

Tip Box

White lighting
To white light myself, Q*i*, people I love, my home or my car I picture an octahedron – two square-based pyramids joined at the base. I begin at the top vertex and picture each side coming down like a transparent blind. Once I have drawn each side of the first pyramid I do the same for the bottom facing pyramid. As I am doing so I claim that I am protecting the person or item out of love. I call upon the energies available to me to protect my loved ones and belongings. And then I trust that it will do the job.

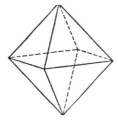

Once I was alone with my daughter, who was aged four at the time, and a cyclone was heading our way. I white lighted the railway carriages I was living in, (I had them on a hectare property in North Queensland – more about those in an appendix), and I could hear the wind hitting something above and beyond my walls. The next morning, I went out to inspect the property in the remainder of the rain and I had about one hundred trees that had fallen over. Every single one of them had fallen outwards and away from the carriages. I was amazed with how effective my white lighting was. There was physical evidence of it. Otherwise how else could I explain the positioning of the trees?

Another time I was travelling through Mexico on a big coach when I realised half way through the trip that I hadn't white lighted the vehicle. I quickly attended to it and within five minutes we had an emergency stop at about 80km/hr and stopped within metres of an oncoming truck. Everyone stopped around us and we had to return to our own lane at a snail's pace. All the passengers were amazed that we'd managed to avoid a crash. I wasn't.

We also have a beautiful guardian angel on the boat who introduced herself to me as Serena. My Maltese friend told me that this means mermaid in her language. That fitted as we were on our way to Malta. Serena communicates with me and warns me when something is going to go wrong. She also told me that I'm not to warn Thomas because it was about him getting used to dealing with emergencies to become a more confident captain. So she tends to let me know the general area where there will be a problem but doesn't tell me exactly. On our first crossing to Sardinia she introduced herself and told me there will be a problem at the back of the boat. I became concerned about the rudder but she wouldn't give any details. She was just letting me know so I could support Thomas if something happened. We arrived in Sardinia at about 2300 and the wind had died down. I was on watch and I checked with Thomas if I could turn on the engine. I did and we didn't move. "Oh, it looks like we've lost the propeller," I stated in surprise. Thomas shook his head and refused to believe it. He tried to check on a few things inside the boat until finally he got the torch and checked underneath. "Yep," he said. "Yep what?" I enquired. "Yep, we've lost the propeller." It took an hour to contact the coast guard by VHF and the whole time I was able to stay calm because I'd been pre-warned and knew we were safe. There was no wind and no propulsion. We rocked like crazy. It was another 45 minutes before the local coast guard arrived. Then it took four hours to tow us into a harbour. We spent another five days organising another propeller. We made the local papers. My pre-warning had assisted me in remaining calm so I could be of assistance.

Checking the vibe of wherever you are is like running your own risk assessment. Each time you have all of your gear in one place you risk something being stolen or losing something of importance. Packing your bag well and ensuring all the zips are done up properly will help to avoid this. Always carry your passport in the bag that you give most attention to and is never out of your sight. Count the number of bags you are carrying continuously and ensure your passport and main wad of cash is well secured. Some people suggest you spread your cash out amongst your gear and have a 'false' wallet with a few old cards, preferably not with your name on them, and a bit of money that you can hand over without losing everything if you get held up. Handbags need to be kept in sight when you go out and I often wrap mine around a table leg before placing it on my lap during a meal or a drink. This deters opportunist snatchers.

I've only ever had one bag stolen and that was in Belgium but I got it back straight away. It was like a scene out of a movie. I was travelling with my seven year old daughter Sam, when a girl from behind started yelling in different languages. I think she tried Flemish first, then French then English. That's when I turned. "That guy just grabbed your backpack!" she yelled. I had been focusing on encouraging Sam to walk to the hostel as I didn't have any local money yet to catch a taxi from the train station. It was just before the introduction of the Euro. I looked in front of me where the young girl was pointing and it was like in slow motion. Some men were bringing a lounge out of a furniture shop and the would-be thief ran into it, rolled over the top of it and threw my bag in the air back at me as he ran off. The bag only had Sam's Barbie dolls and a pair of shoes but she wouldn't have been happy if she'd lost it. I'd had the bag balancing on top of a large suitcase that I was wheeling. Usually I would wrap the straps around a few times, but I mustn't have on this occasion. The young man took the opportunity when I was distracted. I've learned to at least try to act alert.

Your risk assessment involves looking around at the people surrounding you, looking at the quality of the buildings and options for removing yourself safely without a fuss from a situation. Any situation. Keep a good eye on your belongings and don't leave them with anyone you don't know. It's strange how people tend to go into dangerous situations instead of making a fuss. Sometimes you just have to make a fuss. Apologise later for over reactions. Make your next move based on that assessment.

If it looks like there may be a potential danger around you, work out a strategy immediately to remove yourself and get somewhere safe, next to a police officer, back to the hostel, somewhere where there are officials. Even with officials, try to keep someone else with you. Ask for someone else to be present if you are taken to an official's office. You have rights as a human being to consider your own safety. Tell the officer you feel uncomfortable with that arrangement and could someone else attend also.

Tip Box

Identifying the possible dangers in a situation and even discussing them, does not necessarily bring those dangers into your life. However, focusing on them usually will. Yes, assess the dangers but don't let fear drive you.

When I was leaving Cusco an official grabbed my luggage off the scales at the airline's counter and my passport out of the hand of the young attendant. He was speaking Spanish and I didn't understand. I asked the girl what was going on and she said I needed to follow him to his office. He was way out in front of me with my passport and most of my belongings. I caught up to him to walk confidently beside him. I was quickly assessing the situation and realised he had limited English and with my limited Spanish I decided to lag back when he went to enter his office. I showed him that I was hesitant about going in so I stood at the door until I could see other officials and other people being searched. He gestured for me to follow when he realised I wasn't comfortable with the situation. He went to the side and got a female attendant to assist him in his search. I entered the office. The two of them went through all of my bags keeping everything folded. They sniffed everything. I was so glad I'd just done my washing the day before. Once he was finished, he took my luggage back to the counter and gave my passport back to the young girl, wished me well and was on his way. Act confident as though you have nothing to hide and make sure that you're not carrying anything on board a flight that you shouldn't.

Sometimes we are unaware of the dangers lurking. We're just too busy to pick up on the vibe. I had just walked over the Golden Gate Bridge and was walking through the leafy suburb of Presidio when I was faced with a dilemma. It was broad daylight and I looked up ahead and thought, "Hmm, that's a big dog. Hang on, it looks like a wolf, or is it a coyote? Okay, do coyotes attack and eat people? Hmm. Not sure—only sure that they eat road runners. What should I do? Well, in Whistler they said to tell the bears to shoo and go away. Maybe that will work." By this time the coyote had spotted me and was trotting towards me. I puffed myself up and told it that he was a bad dog and to go home. I had resorted to my strategy of dealing with stray dogs coming at me. The coyote continued towards me. I tried again. No response. Third time lucky. He ran off down a small gully. Just then a council truck pulled up beside me and the guy told me that he'd turned around, (what, a car drove past and I never even noticed), to warn me about the coyote. I proudly told him that I'd sent that coyote packing. "Okay," he said and drove away with me watching after him wishing he'd offered me a ride out of there. What if the coyote was packing with others to come in for the kill? Anyway,

I got out of there without any more drama and made my way to Haight-Ashbury. The moral of the story is: always stay confident or act like you are.

I made up my mind that I wouldn't go out on my own at night unless the hostel had a bar or a restaurant either in it or nearby. This worked well as I would usually find someone to join me if I really felt like a night out. However, one night, again in San Francisco, I stayed too long at a sports bar chatting to a funny couple and it was dark outside by the time I was ready to leave. My hostel was in the middle of a park nearby and I didn't feel comfortable walking there alone and a taxi would have had to take the long way around to get there. A group of about six young guys, from the shadier side of life, were just ahead of me walking in the same direction as me. A quick risk assessment helped me decide what to do. I raced up to them and asked if I could walk with them because I wasn't feeling too safe. They loved my accent and asked where I was from. Instantly the vibe changed and I knew I was safe. They were really happy I'd chosen them to protect me and they walked me all the way to the hostel chatting away about Australian animals. It was my gut instinct to make that call and that strategy might not work all the time but it certainly did then. Trust your gut instinct—it's a recognition of the vibe, and don't put yourself in deliberate danger. You can say quite openly that you don't like the vibes there.

Safety Tips for Women Travelling Alone

Be aware of any restrictions about travelling on your own in particular countries as well as any codes of behaviour. For instance there are several Middle-Eastern countries that strictly forbid a woman to travel on her own and some islander cultures in the Pacific have certain codes of dress and behaviour for women. You may only be able to stay by invitation of the elderly women of a group. These are usually off the beaten track places but do your research before you leave for your destination.

The important thing when travelling alone is that you project an air of confidence. Chat with others around you so it that it doesn't look like you're alone. Try to share taxis to and from the airport or use a taxi provided by your accommodation. Taxi drivers have been known to be the attackers in some countries. Know the route that you're meant to be taking so you are able to question any deviation from the set course. At night, always find someone to go out with from the hostel where you're staying and don't travel too far from your accommodation. If you do find yourself out later at night than predicted, join others for any taxi rides or walk within a group. Pretend to be talking on the phone if there isn't suitable company in the vicinity. It doesn't hurt to know some self-defence moves but you have to be prepared to use them. If you find that you're being followed, try to duck into an open business and ask for them to call you a taxi. Avoid carrying large amounts of money or wearing flashy jewellery. Know where you are going and stay in busy streets rather than down any quiet alleys. Don't put yourself at risk unnecessarily and pay attention to the vibe of a place.

Temptations Along the Way

Many opportunities will come your way concerning romance and party times. Be alert and always, ALWAYS be aware of your surroundings and calculating and assessing the risks within them. You're away from home and maybe away from friends that you can rely on. If you must be a party animal, then make sure you trust a 'Party Buddy' to assist you but remember that ultimately you are always responsible for yourself. Make sure you are close to where you're staying or you always have enough cash to get a taxi back there on your own. Drugs are readily available in a lot of countries but fines or imprisonment can seem over the top and consequences can be fatal. I have never indulged in any illegal substances so I'm not about to preach to anyone about the dangers but please be aware of them before you try something you've never touched before. Know the physical effects of any substances and understand where you can obtain medical assistance if needed. Make sure you can rely on a system that can assist you in an emergency. Mainly, be aware of who you are with and your surroundings. Do a risk assessment and make an intelligent decision. I say again and emphasise, do a risk assessment and make an intelligent decision.

Try to lock up your passport and only carry a photocopy of the main page and the page with the entry stamp for the particular country that you're in when you go out or away from your hostel. You may need to carry the real thing in some countries so check when you enter the country about what is required. If you must carry it with you, keep it in a waist belt when you go out and enough money for the evening but no more. Go out with a friend or someone from the hostel.

It goes without saying to keep your drink in your hand and to keep an eye on it. Take care trying local drinks from friendly strangers. I was in Iquitos once and this girl gave the young guy that I'd gone out for a walk with a glass of 'jungle whiskey'. He instantly thought he'd been poisoned and asked me to ask him to do things to see if he would follow my commands without question. He didn't and was relieved that he hadn't been drugged but he said the drink was bloody awful.

As far as the romance goes, take care of your heart and your body. Be prepared to protect your heart and say hello, goodbye and thank them for entering your world for a short time. Taking care of your body and practising safe sex is always important. No matter where you are. Be open for something more serious but be realistic too. I was lucky to find a life-long travel buddy on my travels but at the time I didn't think that it would be anything other than a wonderful holiday romance.

It didn't take long for me to realise that I was falling pretty hard for my captain and saying goodbye would be difficult. It was so fortunate that on the eleventh fantastic day of being with him that he made known that he felt the same way too. We were lazing out on the front deck under the stars and he asked me to just keep sailing with him and never leave his boat. My heart melted although I didn't say yes straight away. He'd been loving my cooking. I had made this fantastic lasagne and I thought, "Oh, my goodness. He's going to want to marry me when he tastes this lasagne." So at the time of his proposal I was thinking, "Heck is this the lasagne talking or him. Oh, my, I put a love spell on the lasagne." I was busy working out how I would have to fly home and sell my car and give gear away to do this . . . and get another year of leave at least from work. The next night we went out to dinner. We were in a small town in Sicily when I said, "You realise I have to go home and sort my life out first." He smiled and said, "So that's a YES." He kissed me passionately and then purchased all the roses from a guy wandering through the summer crowd selling flowers from his garden. I was a goner.

Spell-binding Vegetable Lasagne Recipe

Ingredients

White Sauce
¼ cup of white plain flour
2 cups of milk
75g of butter
½ cup of grated cheddar cheese
1 vegetable stock cube

Tomato Sauce
1 can of diced tomatoes
2 tablespoons of tomato paste
2 teaspoons of sugar
150g of mushrooms
2 grated carrots
1 onion
1 clove of garlic
2 teaspoons of oregano or basil
1 vegetable stock cube

Vegetables and Layers
Any vegetables available
Sliced potato
Sliced sweet potato
Sliced egg plant
Zucchini
Sliced long ways
Silver beet or spinach
A packet of lasagne sheets
More grated cheese to your liking

Method

White Sauce
1. Melt the butter in a saucepan over a low heat.
2. Mix in the flour.
3. Add the milk slowly while still stirring.
4. Continue to stir until thick.
5. Add stock cube and cheese.
6. Remove from heat and place to one side.

Tomato Sauce
1. Fry onion, garlic and sliced mushrooms for 5 minutes.
2. Add the remainder of the ingredients and cook for 10 minutes.
3. Remove from heat and set aside.

Layers and Vegetables
1. Fry all vegetables lightly in oil.
2. Remove and set aside.
3. When everything else is ready boil enough lasagne sheets for one layer for 5 minutes.
4. Begin layering with 1/2 the vegetables on the bottom.
5. Place lasagne sheets and sprinkle with cheese.
6. Boil the next layer of lasagne sheets.
7. Place a layer of white sauce.
8. Continue until you have used up all the ingredients.
9. Bake in an oven for forty minutes at 180 degrees Celsius.

Never underestimate your ability to cope with dangerous situations. Trust that you are safe, be cautious but don't fear what you can't control. Don't put yourself in obviously risky situations. Trust strangers, but not by handing over control of your situation to them. Trust the Universe and that you will be safe, but be responsible for your own actions.

Notes

Action

Do you want to know who you are? Don't ask. Act! Action will delineate and define you.

—Thomas Jefferson

THINKERS ARE CERTAINLY needed in this world to help us develop new ways of doing things and for finding alternative solutions to the world's ills, but there's nothing like putting a plan into action to get a real sense of success.

If you have done a thorough job in your preparation, the timing is right and you're well and excited—it's time to go.

The important thing is to get out there and to do it. Be an action person. Do what you say you're going to do and be a person who people can trust and someone who they can believe in. Walk your talk, as the saying goes. Open your eyes up to this beautiful world and to your beautiful unique soul and journey in this world. Learn what you can about yourself. Explore your comfort zone and outside of it. Pick up on the vibes continuously and act upon them and enjoy. Take care of the environment, tread lightly with it and others. Leave a lasting imprint of hope, love and joy.

A ship is always safe at the shore—but that is NOT what it is built for.

—Albert Einstein

Part 2

TRAVEL STORIES—SNIPPETS OF stories that have happened along the way on my life's journey in no particular order. Sometimes they have a little message and I guess some were just worthwhile sharing. I hope you enjoy them.

Six Degrees of Separation

It's a small world at times and the theory that claims we have only six or less chances of meeting anyone in the world through an introduction is so true. If you talk long enough to someone in any country, you will discover your six degrees or less. I remember being in Queenstown, New Zealand, when a student who did all my sound and lighting for my end of year productions, called out from across the street, "Hi, Ms Morgan." Other students have caught up with me in other parts of the state, one at 4 a.m. at a bus station. Neighbours have been sitting in the row behind me on a plane when there's been an unrelated starting point or destination—it was a connecting flight for both of us. A sailor we met in Colombia used to be married to one of my ex-husband's friends. Another couple we met along the way was sailing in a boat that an ex-boyfriend had built. So, always remember that you are who you are and you are in your skin for your whole life. Don't go thinking that any of your antics are isolated from you as a person. Don't do anything that will come back to haunt you under the guise that you're a long way from home.

Bucket List

Ensure you are ticking off those 'must do' items for yourself as you travel through life. Having quite a number of trips under my belt now, my bucket list is slowly getting ticked off, yet new items are being added along the way. When I was eleven, it was my mum's bucket list item that took us to the centre of Australia to climb Uluru— Ayers Rock as it was called back then. It was her life's ambition, as she put it. It has always been inappropriate to climb the rock but there was a lot less social awareness and pressure encouraging one to be culturally sensitive to the original custodians of the land back in the early 70's.

We'd arrived late in the afternoon after our journey from Alice Springs and we were all too excited to sleep. Once we had our camp site set up, Dad took us for a drive around the base of the rock. He pulled up at the section where the climbing route began and laughed at quite a number of bronze plaques imprinted on the side of the walking track. "Those are all the memorial plaques for people who had died on the rock," he teased our mother. The three of us kids raced up the rock to the inscriptions, only to find that he was right. Quite a number of people had suffered heart attacks, fallen off the rock or experienced other fatal circumstances whilst climbing the rock. One plaque stated that it was the gentleman's life ambition to climb the rock and he'd fulfilled that dream. He'd died of a heart attack somewhere up the top. We all looked at Mum concerned for her mortal safety. We all survived the climb, although it was a lot windier than what I thought it would be. I could understand how people actually met their demise as we were nearly blown away. I've never heard Mum mention again that she had any more life ambitions but I certainly want to keep adding things to my list.

I've listed my top bucket list items that I've enjoyed already or am still enjoying. Some people have activities on their list that stretch them to their limits like climbing to Base Camp or parachuting. I have only had a few of these. I'm a bit kinder to my body. I'm often in it for the spiritual experience.

1. Walk the Inca Trail.
2. Visit England and roaming the countryside.
3. Visit Pompeii.
4. Visit the Tower of London.
5. Fly over the Nasca Lines.
6. Take a boat trip into the Amazon and see the pink dolphins.
7. Walk into an active volcano.
8. Swim with the humpbacks in Tonga.
9. Blackwater rafting through the Waitomo Caves.
10. Sail around the world.
11. Visit Russia.
12. Sail in the Mediterranean.
13. Cruise the Nile.
14. Visit the Valley of the Kings.
15. Visit Delphi in Greece.
16. Cruise around the Fjords of Norway.
17. Camp under the Northern Lights.

There are probably still another twenty or so things that I would really like to do but seeing the Aurora Borealis is probably number one on my list, and as we're usually cruising in tropical zones, I don't think I'll get it done any time soon. Make the list and enjoy adding/deleting as you find more wonders in the world.

Becoming Accustomed to it

Going through Customs and Quarantine can be quite arduous if you're travelling through a lot of different countries. The best way to operate is to avoid souvenirs that you will need to declare. For example: avoid Mexican jumping beans. Know your own country's intricacies before you leave. Some items may need fumigation upon return and this could cost more than what the item is worth or the Department of Agriculture destroys it. We bought some drums in Dominica and when we arrived in Australia with the yacht the quarantine guys inspected them and discovered that they still had goat hair on the skin. They both had to be fumigated at a cost of AUD$100. They were worth a lot more than that so we didn't hesitate. In some South American countries there is a random selection of travellers identified by a red or green light. If it turns red for you, all your items are thoroughly checked. I wasn't concerned when I flew into Peru because I thought I had nothing to declare. Later unpacking my backpack I discovered an uneaten packet of biscuits that I had forgotten about. This would have been enough to land a huge fine if I'd been selected. It was purely by accident but it always pays to double check the contents of your bag. Needless to say—Just don't ever carry anything that could land you in dire trouble. Just don't risk it.

Scottish Monsters

I was driving through Scotland with my mum and daughter when my 'very down to earth' mother says upon seeing a large dolphin surfacing in a loch beside the road, "Oh look! It's the Loch Ness Monster . . . Oh it can't be. That loch isn't Loch Ness." I had to laugh at the idea that she was actually keeping an eye out for Nessie. You just never know your luck when you're in places where legends originate.

Aztecs and Abductions

On the advice of my friends in the U.S. rather than driving on my own, I joined a tour through Mexico and it turned out to be fantastic. There were eight of us with a young Mexican guide. All our accommodation and transport were included and our guide took us to local quality restaurants where we could get the speciality of the area for a reasonable cost. We visited the various Aztec sites from Mexico City to Cancun.

Half-way through our journey when we were visiting the town of Palenque to see the Mayan ruins in the rainforest, our guide went missing. I knew something was wrong but my travelling companions kept trying to convince me otherwise. They thought that he was just resting. Eventually he reappeared to tell us the story of how he had been abducted at gun point by three masked men in a white van. There were three other captives already held hostage when our guide was forced into the van near a roundabout, just after visiting the ATM. After relieving the men of their wallets and phones, the abductors drove them to the high cliffs of the fast running river about thirty minutes out of town. The abductees were ordered to jump the twenty or so metres into the water. Our guide described how he stayed under the water, swimming with the current because he was afraid that the abductors would begin shooting into the water. He wasn't even sure if the water would be deep enough for them to survive the jump but obviously it was. They floated down river, climbed up on the bank and ended up hitch hiking back to town. Luckily our guide new the area quite well and they made it back to town safely from their four hour ordeal. It's always a good idea to visit an ATM with someone else if you're in a dodgy area, even if you're a local.

Coyote Circuit

(Story is in Part 1 too)

Planning a combination of a walking/bus tour incorporating local buses can make for an inexpensive day out. Having mapped out a circuit of walking around the bay of San Francisco amongst all the exercising fanatics, across the Golden Gate Bridge, through the Prescido neighbourhood and onward by bus to Haight-Ashton and then returning to my hostel in the park back on the bay, I set out for a big day out. I relished in watching the busy pace of life of the locals and the boats on the bay. Crossing the Golden Gate Bridge was a triumph and I was both amused and saddened at the same time by the signs everywhere encouraging you to phone a number if the impulse to jump got too strong. I wondered if the signage had ever worked and some sad soul had actually rung that number. After returning back across the bridge, in awe of the sights of the city, I continued through the leafy ex-military suburb of Prescido.

Winding through the streets, I made my way to a road where I could get a bus to my next destination. The terrain seemed to turn more rural as I walked along a road edging a small bushy gully. I stopped abruptly when a large dog ahead of me caught my sight. Simultaneously, he delighted in noticing me. It took a moment for my brain to register the type of dog I was gazing upon. As it began to trot towards me, the inner safety bells began tinkering slightly. Upon realisation that it was a coyote, my brain seemed to run through my memory banks like a slot machine attempting to recall any clue about what the correct procedure was when faced with this wild animal.

Having no recollection, I referred to my brain file about wild bears in Canada. Tell them to shoo. So with a combination of my usual action when being approached by a mean dog and the wild bear response, I told him that he was a bad dog and that he should shoo. Convinced that I must have either had food or was a tasty morsel, he kept on trotting towards me without a change of pace. Only after the third attempt of deterring him did he turn and run down into the gully. Proud of my ability to maintain my composure, and talk to dogs, I looked about and continued on my way, just looking over my shoulder to keep a check on my rear guard. A council truck pulled up with a guy warning me to watch out for the coyote that he just saw running down into the gully. I proudly told him that I'd sent that coyote packing and he drove on but with me wishing I had asked him for a lift out of there.

Serena our Guide on the Sea

It wasn't long after Thomas and I began our first overnight crossing to Sardinia when Serena presented herself to me. Visually she has the face of an imp and only the upper part of her body really takes form with a wispy sheer cloth blowing in the wind. She tends to fly around the rear of the boat above us. Her tangled fine brown hair flows as freely as the rest of her. She is a delicate picture of beauty, and still she radiates protection and power. Her messages are mixed in the way that she identifies situations before they occur, asks me not to mention them to Thomas but forewarns me by showing me a location on the boat where the trouble will occur. Her initial warning was in regard to something at the rear of the boat. She advised me to stay calm because we would be safe. She wouldn't let anything happen to us but she wanted Thomas to gain confidence in handling emergencies. He was still pretty new to sailing.

It wasn't until we arrived in amongst the southern islands of Sardinia and the wind became confused, that we attempted to motor. It was late at night and it was on my shift. It had become difficult to maintain our course winding through the channel to the anchorage that Thomas had chosen. Islands and points on land mess with the wind direction when you are close. However, when I engaged the engine, nothing happened.

I immediately said that it seemed like the propeller had fallen off. The look of disbelief from Thomas made me wonder if I was far off the mark. He checked the shaft and figured that something was amiss but he would sail on and then look at it in the light of day. It was a dark moonless night and Thomas wasn't attracted to the idea of going into the black water to check things.

It was only a few hours later that the wind had totally gone and we were bobbing wildly about on some mean little waves. Everything below was rolling around from side to side. The plates and pots were crashing about. Resigned to the fact that he would have to take the plunge, Thomas discovered that we had in fact lost the propeller. With no means of propulsion, we were at the mercy of the currents and waves. We were drifting towards a small island that we could see on the charts but not before us through the darkness. We decided that we needed to call a 'pan pan', which is an emergency call without the urgency of a life and death situation. We continued to bob around helplessly as it took over an hour for someone to respond.

Once we had finally reached the local coast guard, we had to wait another forty-five minutes for them to arrive. So in broken English, my German captain and our Italian rescuers communicated and we were on our way being towed safely into harbour. I was grateful for Serena's warning as it prepared me for the situation. There was no panic, just calm suggestions that lead to a favourable outcome.

Mission Impossible

Losing your propeller in the month of August in Italy is not advisable. August is a month of celebrations, when the businesses are shut down and everyone is at play. However, we were able to arrange a replacement but it needed to be modified. Thomas had to dive into the filthy water of the harbour on five different occasions to measure and inspect the shaft before he could actually fit the new propeller. This all happened over a course of seven days.

On the fifth dive, an official from the Coast Guard wandered over to check on us and ask us how it was going. Thomas emerged from the harbour in his scuba gear and the look of horror on the official's face was evidence enough that we had done something wrong. He flapped his arms around and yelled at us in Italian until he realised that we were baffled by his outrage. Upon finding his English he told us in an elevated tone that this was IMPOSSIBLE. Only it was stretched out into extra-long syllables—eem-possss-eeee-beele. Thomas assured him that it wouldn't happen again. Thank goodness we'd just managed to fit the propeller. The official's outrage became our catch cry for whenever anything was difficult. "Eem-possss-eeee-beele!"

Seemingly Innocent Crocodiles

We had a visitor come on board when we were cruising around Jamaica who was keen to go on the crocodile tour when we arrived in Black River. We'd gone to shore in the afternoon and had rafted our dinghy to a tour boat at the crocodile tour office. There was a great plastic crocodile on the corner of the dock and I begged Thomas to park near it so we could get a photo of it guarding the dinghy. Reluctant to just park the dinghy anywhere, Thomas asked an obvious worker where he could tie up. I was disappointed that he advised us to raft up to one of their tour boats. We tied up as per instructions, we went into town to get some provisions and upon our return we booked a crocodile tour for the following day. The next morning, I was disenchanted to see that the crocodile hadn't been put out yet. Even on our return from our tour, it still wasn't there.

Our visitor and I went on another tour up into the hills via local taxis to visit some waterfalls while Thomas went and did some maintenance on the boat. Upon our return we saw the crocodile had finally been put out. I encouraged our visitor towards it and said how much fun it would be to get our photos taken with our heads inside its wide-open mouth. 'Nah, she replied, "I'll just put my hand in." So we went to go up to it for the photo shoot when it moved its head from side to side and then froze. Amazed at the sophistication of this remote controlled beast, I turned to a man standing there in uniform and accusingly said, "You did that." He shook his head adamantly, held his hands up in surrender and said he'd had nothing to do with it. Not to be taken for a fool, I continued my approach when it really lashed its head about. Hopping back laughing, realising that we had been foolish by not recognising this as a real croc, the man asked us what was so funny. I explained how we'd been determined to get our photos taken with our head and hands in its mouth. Then we went to talk to some tourists and told them how convinced we'd been that it was plastic—it really looked like it. We didn't notice that the man in the uniform had gone inside to tell the owners about these crazy white women who were going to stick their heads and hands into the croc's mouth.

Before this, I had radioed Thomas to collect us. Upon seeing the crocodile on his arrival he headed straight for it so I could get the photo that I'd asked for the day before. I realised what he was doing and madly tried, unsuccessfully, to avert his rapid approach towards the reptile. I couldn't rush towards him because the crocodile was between us, so I just jumped around on the spot yelling and waving my arms for him to stop. Never really paying much attention to my dramatics or being able to hear me over the motor, the captain kept speeding towards his inevitable doom, when suddenly the crocodile turned and lunged towards him and under the dinghy. Then, and only then, the captain realised what I was trying to warn him about. He immediately slowed the dinghy down and the momentum pushed him into the dock. The horrified surprised look on his face was priceless. He tied up and we fell together roaring with laughter with tears in our eyes. Simultaneously, the big woman from the office came out roaring at us about how we were going to destroy the tourism business of Jamaica by being stupid enough to be eaten by a crocodile. We were just laughing too much to stop and she carried on for a bit longer and then threw her arms up in disbelief at the ignorance of tourists and went back inside. For three days, the three of us couldn't look at each other without bursting out laughing at how stupid we'd been.

What Goes Around Comes Around

Having a strong belief in Karma, my love of other humans and enjoying making people smile, leads me towards purposeful rather than random acts of kindness—everyday. It was over the Christmas holidays back on the Gold Coast when I was teaching a young friend of mine how to surf. Upon exiting the water, I was approached by a Canadian guy who asked me if I would teach his son and his son's friend how to surf. He offered me cash. Now not being a very good surfer myself, I thought it would be a bit rude to take his money but I said that I would still teach the boys. He said that was very kind of me and added that he owned a place in Whistler, Canada and if I ever happened to be over there, I was welcome to visit. The boys turned out to be young men who were ski instructors. They also invited me to go to Whistler to learn how to ski. Over New Years, at the beginning of my big journey, I ended up spending a week staying with them, getting discounts on ski hire and lift passes and enjoying the slopes. It was an amazing exchange of energy for having a good time and teaching some keen young men a new sport.

Another time I offered to clean up some pots and pans for a lady in a hostel so that she could enjoy her meal while it was hot. I was just standing around waiting for some of my food to cook, so it wasn't any bother. We got talking and she was from Aspen and she invited me to visit her there. I didn't get the chance to take her up on her offer but it is still there and she didn't get me to clean up the pans. It just became a starting point for a conversation.

Even though I don't expect anything in return, it is always amazing when it does.

Avoid Moscow Airport on the Weekend

I was travelling with my mum and two other friends when we arrived in Moscow on a Friday night. Apparently half of Eastern Europe arrives then too on the weekend getaway deals. It was during a heatwave in the summer of 2010. There was no air conditioning in the building and there were about two thousand unruly, sweaty, smelly, weary travellers packed into an area the size of half a basketball court. People were backed up the stairway. Babies were screaming and old people were praying. No officials were in sight except for the few in the safety of their booths that lined the exit to the luggage collection and the outside world.

Random people were pushing in all over the place. Disgruntled elderly women were calling out their dismay at the rudeness of these mannerisms. Even my mum got in on the show. It took two hours to get through immigration only to discover that about 10 aircraft's worth of luggage was strewn around, and in between four conveyor belts. I ended up leaping, as lady-like as possible, over the belts and into the centre to retrieve our bags. Then calls came from all around to grab other people's luggage for them. I continued for about five minutes before I deserted my post because we were already about an hour late meeting our chaperones. We had dramas leaving St. Petersburg on a Friday night too, so decided that the weekend was a bad time to travel in Russia.

Personal Safety Siren

When we arrived in Manchester early 2001 for my teaching stint, I was given a personal alarm as some members of our teaching group were concerned for their own safety in this big town. This ended up coming in handy when my daughter, who was seven at the time, and I were travelling through Paris. We had quite a few pieces of luggage because of all the gear we'd accumulated over the seven months we lived in England and I was on my way back to Australia.

I was at the northern railway station to catch a train to Belgium when I realised that I didn't have a clue where the right platform was. There seemed to be multi-levels and I was absolutely confused. I was running out of time before our train would leave. Exhausted from dragging all the luggage and a complaining child around, I set her up with all the gear and dashed down an elevator to quickly check the screen on a different floor. I gave her the safety alarm and told her to set it off if she felt endangered in any way. I would only be gone two minutes. Upon my return I found a crowd of people around her but maintaining a healthy distance. There she was perched on top of the pile of luggage holding the screaming alarm. She had wanted to test it.

Mountain Biking to Swimming with Sharks

We stopped over in the Galapagos Islands on our crossing of the Pacific Ocean in 2014 and found it rather expensive. Determined to see one of the islands, we hired two mountain bikes and set out for a tour of some lava caves and up to a crater of an extinct volcano. At the lava caves we were met by a delightful woman, Stella. With limited English, she fussed over us and made us feel welcome. She organised bananas and an ice cream for us and ensured we understood the trek through the caves. She was motherly and kind. She hugged us as we began our journey through the caves as if we were her long lost children. Upon our return she gave us a drink and reluctantly sent us on our way.

Our next stop was the top of a small hill which was actually the rim of a volcano. In amongst the clouds, with a limited view, we ate lunch and then began our steep descent. As the hire bikes had dodgy brakes, I decided to take it very easy. I told Thomas that I would meet him at the shop at the bottom but being the gentleman that he is, he told me we'd wait for me every kilometre or less. As I was coming down, I spotted a huge long pothole expanding the width of the road. Pushing extra hard, I had inadvertently used the front brakes causing the bike to come to an abrupt halt. As I flew through the air over the handlebars, in what seemed like slow motion, I was thinking, 'this isn't going to be good.' My loose fitting helmet rolled off and my face collected gravel from the road. I slid along with my bike for about a metre.

Lying there in the middle of the road, feeling numb and unable to move, I began to call feebly to Thomas. Realising that something must be amiss, Thomas was already returning to see where I was. He rushed up to me and tried to get me to move but when he saw that I was only a bit scratched up and muddied, he thought it was a great opportunity for a photo shoot and he had a good laugh. Not so gentlemanly after all!

I was in pain and miserable and we were still about nine kilometres from the boat harbour. I just wanted to return to Stella's loving arms so she could tend my wounds. Thomas told me it was too far back uphill to get to her so I would have to tough it out and ride back to the boat. Covered in mud and blood, we rode through town and dropped the bikes off. We headed for the dock to return to the boat when everyone was pointing towards the hospital and telling Thomas to take me there. He told them in Spanish that I would be alright. I limped along behind him wondering if I really was. We got back to the boat where we had about fourteen black tip reef sharks circling. I think they could already smell my blood. At least Thomas dived in to scare them away before I hopped in to wash all the blood and mud off! Okay, points back on for being a gentleman.

Conwy Castle

It was an easy drive from Manchester over into northern Wales to the beautiful ancient town of Conwy. The ruins of the old castle built between 1283 and 1289 by Edward the First, were full of energies from the past. When I put my hand into one of the old ovens, in what used to be the kitchen, it tingled and sparked away. As I walked into one of the rooms on the ground floor, in my mind's eye, I could see the king dancing in a private embrace with his queen. At that moment, a minute whirly-wind moved about on the dust. It almost appeared to be moving in time to some forgotten tune. The spinning dust remained for a few minutes as an influx of images and feelings were bestowed upon me. There was a lot of love between the king and the queen and I could feel it. I later purchased a booklet about the castle and upon examination of the plan I discovered that it had been the king's bed chambers where I had seen the whirly-wind and received those images. I love getting pictures from spirit.

Navigating by the Sun

When Mum and I went to Greece in 2007, we hired a small car and tripped around the Peloponnese and along to Delphi. I drove and Mum navigated. Every day, we would get lost but we managed to always reach our destination, eventually. On the last day, we needed to drop the car back at the airport but I'd found the exit signs confusing and missed our turn off the motorway. I took the next turn off and I went to ask Mum if I should just . . . no she had it all figured out immediately. She had the map and she directed me down and up different secondary streets. It took us a while but we ended up on the road to the airport. She proudly exclaimed how she had followed the sun to work out which direction we should be heading in. I told her that I was just going to get back on the highway, going back the way we came and take the correct exit. Deflated, she responded with yes, we could've done that too and it may have been a lot easier.

York in England

I would have to say that York is one of my favourite places in England. I ended up visiting it four times while I was living in Manchester. The ghost tour was fascinating and this is where history really came alive for me—so to speak. I was so confused with the order that the different conquests had occurred in England but seeing the time line on the stairway at the hostel there, just helped it all make so much sense. The 'shambles', the old butcher's houses, were so picturesque. It truly is a beautiful town with a colourful and interesting history. History, ghosts and living history through architecture—the place is a treat.

Iquitos in the Jungle

Probably the scariest place on any of my journeys was Iquitos, Peru. I had just flown to Lima from Cusco after the four day hike to Machu Picchu and after a five hour stopover in Lima, I had flown to Iquitos. I had been taken aside for a search in Cusco and wasn't sure if I would make my flight. It had been a long day and I hadn't had the chance to research how far I had to go from the airport to my hostel. That was something I always tried to do so I could work out a fair price for a taxi. So I was feeling a little bit vulnerable when I left the airport into the thick humid air to be faced with a horde of taxi drivers yelling prices at me.

They were calling out in broken English and I would have probably understood them better if they had been speaking in Spanish. All of a sudden, one fellow called out ten dollars and I said that would be fine. He grabbed my suitcase and as he headed off, a man called after me, "No, no, don't go with him. He psycho. He psycho." As the other driver had already disappeared with my luggage, I turned to follow him, asking myself what I had gotten myself into. When I reached his vehicle, I realised what the other guy was trying to tell me. Okay, a 'motorpsycho'. The guy was trying to warn me that the taxi driver's vehicle was a motorcycle and that I risked getting wet. It was a 'tri-cycle' with a covered area and two seats.

I relaxed briefly but then noticed the rain beginning. The driving was erratic and we zoomed under a covered area, which was like an old petrol station. My driver told me to wait there in the vehicle. After about fifteen minutes, I decided I really needed to get moving.

I was exhausted and wanted to get to bed. I got my poncho out of my bag and covered myself and my gear and asked my driver to get moving again. I arrived at the Floating hostel only to find that the boards leading out to it were partially submerged. The torrential tropical rain had eased slightly at least. I arrived in the floating bar and reception area. There were hammocks, psychedelic pictures and groups of relaxed people hanging everywhere. A kind lady appeared and looked quizzically at me. I informed her that I had a booking and she told me that their internet had been down and they hadn't received it. She showed me a room which was partly submerged and said that I had a choice of that one on my own or a mixed room that only had a top bunk available. I figured I was safer on the top bunk as the person below would wake me up if we began to sink. I can sleep through anything.

After moving my gear into the dorm, I returned to the bar for a beer and met some of the other guests. I was immediately offered some drugs which I declined. One young fellow asked me if I'd like to take a walk through town to check it out. Even though I was rather exhausted, I had gotten a second wind and was keen to work out where I actually was in the world.

I found the streets hazy with the steam and filled with all sorts of characters from all walks of life. There was an eerie vibe in the town. Drugs were obviously a big part of the culture here and anywhere where that is the case, there is an unknown quantity of risk. People become unpredictable with such chemical imbalances in their bodies. I am not one to live in fear but I was certainly concerned for my safety in this town. I didn't like the vibe and I knew I couldn't leave straight away. I just had to keep myself safe.

Even getting into one of their tri-motorcycles was a risk. I ended up going for an overnight journey into the Amazon and while I was away, two tourists were killed in an accident while travelling in one. However, I would have to conclude that it was the drug culture that made me feel so uncomfortable. It's just not a part of my world. As a human body is meant to resonate at a designed level, any substances that mess with this will cause all the energy to be out of whack.

Gauging people's energy is a big part of how I interact and without it being in harmony with the surroundings, I become confused and uncomfortable. This doesn't mean I would never go to Iquitos again. I would just be more prepared next time. I would probably be more proactive in altering the vibe. It is a gateway into the Amazon and has many amazing sights to see.

Dragon Houses in the Greek Isles

An ancient myth of dragons occupying old slate-roofed houses in the hills on some of the northern islands in Greece, kept would-be explorers at bay. This helped preserve these structures dating back hundreds or even thousands of years.

Part of my big year off was to sail around the Mediterranean. I used the website Find a Crew to locate boats and help meet up with captains who were relaxed and willing to have visitors on board. Contributing my share of the costs and paying a small fee to assist with wear and tear on the boat meant I had a few months touring for under 150 Euro a week. It was a bargain and I met wonderful people along the way.

My second boat took me and my five companions up into the northern islands of Greece and we ended up on Lemnos. The four Italians on board were all friends from Milan and the young Wisconsin man had also joined them through Find a Crew, and then there was me. Each island we came to became an opportunity to explore and we would chip in and hire a car if it appeared to be worthwhile.

I was determined to find some of the dragon houses and the quality of the tourist maps sometimes made this venture very difficult. Much to the horror of the Italian who had signed his name on the hire papers of the first car, I was leading us across country on rugged roads that looked as though they hadn't been repaired since the fall of the Roman Empire. We had aborted several attempts after it looked like our little car was going to be swallowed up by the pot holes but I was determined to see these ancient structures.

Resigned to the fact that the maps just weren't leading us in the right direction on the minor roads, we headed to the other end of the island to explore the landscape. Along the way, we found some of the dwellings just off the main road. There were groups of them in isolated villages scattered around the islands. The walls were made out of rocks and the roofing was cut from large slabs of slate. I don't know how the legend began about dragons living in them but I was enthralled by the prospect of wandering through the houses of a people lost in time. The energies were very tranquil. They made for a great place to meditate and to become a part of the lifestyle that they once had. It became a catch cry for the group that we were off to find the dragon houses.

Nude Beaches and Fast Cars

Part of my journey in 2010 with my mum and two friends led us to the northern German island of Rügen where one of my friends had hoped to find out a bit about her family history. We had flown into Berlin after visiting Russia and picked up a hire car. After exploring Check Point Charlie, the remains of the wall and other sights in Berlin, we headed north on an autobahn to Rügen. I really wanted to experience the speed on the autobahn but a Ford Focus with 4 women and 4 lots of luggage just didn't cut it. I could only push the little car to 160km, which was faster than I'd ever gone in a car before, but it was struggling. I found the most awkward part of the process was being able to gauge how fast the cars were approaching from the rear. What would appear to be a tiny dot in the distance behind us, would soon be a streak of lightning passing us. It was a bit disconcerting when we needed to pass a slow campervan or similar sluggish vehicle.

When we arrived at Rügen we realised that many German holiday-makers were making the most of their summer break. We explored the island and discovered the shell of a hotel that Hitler was having built in the '40s so his soldiers could have some R&R. It was over 3km long and construction was incomplete. This derelict monstrosity had been taken over in some sections by industrious artists and squatters. But in the most part, it had been abandoned. It was a strange sight.

We had read about the amber littered beaches and decided to take a stroll in search of treasures. We were quite surprised by how many nudists there were on the beach. Poor old Mum was looking about and exclaimed that she'd never seen so many penises in her life but she was smiling. We passed a volleyball court in the process of getting set up and our imagination couldn't help but conjure up images of how that scene might look once the game began. It lead to jokes and raucous childish laughter amongst us. We walked a large length of the beach, explored some ruins of the long hotel and visited some artist's galleries before we decided to return to the car. One of us asked if we should walk the beach or take the parallel path back to the car park. Always up for a beach walk I opted for the beach upon which my super sporty mum gleefully exclaimed with a cackle, "Yes, maybe the volleyball game has begun." We all giggled like school girls.

Glowing Dolphins

I know I've put this story elsewhere in my book but in case you missed it, I wanted to share it again.

We were nearly ready to leave the Mediterranean and we were just off the rock of Gibraltar in the early hours of the morning when Thomas called me from my slumber to come up on deck. There in the plankton-rich water was a pod of dolphins dashing under the boat and swimming in the bow wave. All their features were lit up from the glow of the plankton. Their torpedo-like action made them appear like comets dashing through the water. As they leapt and splashed, the droplets of sparkling water seemed suspended in the air. Their playful antics continued for about half an hour before they receded into the depths. It was probably the most magical phenomena I have ever witnessed. Had I known it was possible, I would have put it on my bucket list and sought it out.

Careful what you ask for

On the eve of departure for our Atlantic crossing, I asked the captain how he was feeling and if he was ready for this. He responded affirmatively except he added, "I just wish I'd experienced a storm. I'm just not sure how I'll go in one." The next day we left without pomp and cheer onto one of the biggest adventures of our lives. We'd organised crew for our crossing because we weren't sure how we would handle all the night watches over the next 34 or so days. There was a bit of sheet lightning around in spite of having checked the forecasts and found a good weather window with a good amount of wind. Our crew was battling a bit of sea sickness but soldiered on with their first watch.

Thomas and I had just retired for a few hours when the storm hit. The thunder was rumbling and the lightning was growing in intensity. The crew called for Thomas to come up on deck as the helm was becoming difficult to handle. The lightning was so close that they could see the vibrations of energy hit the sails simultaneously with the boom of thunder. The seas whipped up into a frenzy and we were being tossed about violently. We were surfing down the waves with spray dampening us. We were seeing gusts of 49 knots of wind but Qi, the yacht, handled things well. Her transom lifted gently and pushed us forward down the wave. It was difficult to steer and we had to take care that the boat didn't round up into the wave, putting us side on to the wall of water. The storm continued for three days and we were all quite weary.

On the second day of the storm I was on the helm and I'd received a message from the ethos to expect a huge wave, different from the rest. I was hanging on and concentrating on every movement of the boat and the sea. Thomas was sitting in the cockpit facing me when I saw his eyes grow bigger. I braced myself and a torrent of water pushed me against the helm. I continued to steer and Thomas desperately reached for the cockpit drains to clear the water away. A discarded life jacket had inflated on the floor of the cockpit creating a distraction. We burst out laughing as one of our crew arrived to check on our wellbeing. Thomas quickly instructed him to close some portholes leading down into the cabin to stop the water from going inside.

It took us a few days to wind down from the intensity of the three days but the captain was happy he'd had his storm and that he saw how well the boat had behaved. It still remains to be the worst storm we've experienced at sea. We were very thankful that we had crew to assist us.

First time cooking on rough water

Cooking at anchor is usually a piece of cake on Q*i*. I have everything I need close to hand and it didn't take me long to adapt to the galley. But cooking at sea is a different matter altogether. The first time Thomas took me out of sheltered waters when I was cooking was when we were departing the main harbour of Menorca. Thomas had advised me that it would probably take twenty minutes before we were outside so I could use this time to prepare our lunch.

Unfortunately, it only took about seven minutes and I wasn't ready for the pitching and rolling of the boat. Oranges left the safety of the cardboard, rice showered me like confetti, plastic containers slipped about on the bench and pots flew out as if poltergeists were targeting me. I remember putting everything into the sink and then starting again—methodically.

I now have a refined process where I brace myself between the engine cupboard and the bench. I utilise a combination of a large high-sided tray and non-slip mats. I prepare everything before I turn on the stove. Our gas cooker is gimballed, which means it can swing in time with the boat to keep the contents of the pots at an even level. It's been a long process adapting to cooking in a kitchen where the floor seems to give way but now I can prepare food in the roughest of oceans. It always takes three times longer than cooking in a normal kitchen and it's exhausting.

Carlos el pájaro

It's amazing how many birds visit us on Q*i* but one in particular stands out. We were about sixty km off the coast of Columbia when this small bird appeared in the cockpit of the boat. He fluttered approvingly about the place before he flew downstairs to inspect the amenities. He discovered himself in the mirror and was instantly in love. He stayed with us for about four hours, returning to the cockpit to get some fresh air on occasions. He even landed on Thomas' arm and stayed there looking at him. We named him Carlos and we enjoyed his company. Upon arrival in Santa Marta, where we checked in, he flew upstairs, leisurely inspected his surroundings and then flew off. As Thomas always thought that it would be the birds through the forest that he would miss the most about Germany, it's quite amusing that these feathered friends visit us throughout different times of our travel.

Talking to dogs

Thomas and I are both animal lovers and miss not having pets. We've seen a number of boat dogs and cats and although the animals seem to adapt quite well to their aquatic habitats, we've noticed the amount of complication they produce when checking into new countries. We tend to befriend different animals along the way instead.

When I was a teenager it would take me an extra fifteen minutes to get to work due to the number of animals that would come out of their homes to talk to me and have a smooch. Cats and dogs have often spoken to me. Without communicating directly, I tend to know what most are thinking. Dogs in particular take advantage of this and tell me their ills so I can advise their owners. Most owners are a bit taken aback when I tell them something is up with their pooch. Their first response is usually, "How did you know that?" They don't flinch when I tell them that he or she told me. Most are grateful. For example, a man had a small dog at a pizza restaurant where all the cruisers would eat once a week in Panama City. I approached him as we were leaving to tell him that his dog asked me to ask him if he could modify the dog's diet as his kidneys were suffering with the dried food. The man thanked me profusely because they had just lost their older dog to kidney disease and had modified her diet on advice from the vet but hadn't changed the younger dog's diet. He hadn't thought of it. Dogs make a beeline for both Thomas and I when we're walking down the street. People notice and comment in a humorous way.

As we were walking to a national park in the countryside in Colombia, a young white dog joined us along the road. He trotted beside us as if we were his best mates. He didn't speak to us, just joined us. When we entered the park, we were met by two big dogs and we noticed our four legged friend had left us. We paid our entry fee and continued down a winding path and noticed that our friend had taken a detour and trotted down his own well-worn track to join us again. He showed us the way on different parts of the hike where we had been told we could divert from the main track and visit more waterfalls. We were hesitant at several points, unsure of our direction, when he ran up in front and showed us the way. When we set up the camera for photos, he would run to us and pose with us. He was great company and a real help. Without a farewell, he left us as we exited the park and, I imagine, returned home content from his morning walk. We suspected that this was a regular routine of his, judging from the well-worn detour that he'd taken to avoid the big dogs at the entrance.

Altitudes and Glaciers

If you haven't heard of altitude sickness before and you're on your way to some high altitudes, you might want to read a bit about it. Two nights before I was due to walk the Inca Trail, I developed a weird headache. It felt like bubbles were moving around my brain. Adding nausea to the equation made me quite concerned about my ability to conquer the trail. I was fine the next morning, so I was glad that I'd had an early night and relaxed about the whole situation. Others weren't so lucky. One lady opted out.

This has been my only experience with what was most probably altitude sickness. Even though Thomas and I hiked up to a Glacier at 4700m in Colombia, I remained unaffected. Well maybe not quite unaffected. I got a bit hyperactive, whereas Thomas was rendered almost incapacitated. He was gasping for breath as we left the comfort of the van at the 4100 metre mark and only grew worse as we hiked higher. The vegetation was unique and had us awestruck as it changed the higher we went, so it was still well worth the journey.

Altitude sickness is unpredictable and there's really nothing to do for it except to rest up and avoid alcohol for a few days before and after you arrive. Research any up-to-date information about it. Some people have tried taking tablets but still claim to get it. Others chew leaves off certain plants but everybody is affected differently. Arrive at least two days before any strenuous planned activity so your body has time to adjust. You don't want to have to miss out on a Bucket List item at the last minute.

Upgrades

I don't get upgraded very often but when it happens, it's a wonderful gift. Upgraded flights, in particular, are a joy but even better than that, is an upgrade on a hire car or accommodation. These things last longer and can really add another dimension to your journey. I had a compact car hired in Germany to travel approximately 600km and then realised, on the fine print, that the kilometres weren't included.

I contacted the company and they charged a small amount for the alterations to my booking. Then when we arrived to pick up the car, they had upgraded us again to an Audi 3. This meant that Thomas could really show me his driving skills on the autobahn. It cut time off our journey and created a unique experience.

In Colombia we arrived at a coffee plantation expecting a double room in their hostel. They were a little bewildered by our arrival late in the evening and couldn't find our booking. Yet another case of internet problems. So they upgraded us to the main plantation house for our two day booking. There, we had a housekeeper on hand serving us drinks and cooking us meals. The rooms were decked out with antiques and the wide verandas had hammocks, sitting areas and books. Manicured lawns encompassed an unfenced pool surrounded by deck chairs. We still did our hikes around the area but coming back to this unique place made for unforgettable memories. Sometimes the special details can create a sense of luxury.

Staying in hostels throughout Britain creates a sense of luxury as some of the old estate houses are quite exceptional. In fact, I have been amazed at the establishments throughout the whole world. Sweden has an old jail where you can stay as well as an old ship. Scotland has estate houses with turrets like castles. England has old windmills and barns. You can find your little bit of luxury and upgrades in everything you do. It's about your perceptions and how you alter the vibe.

When Hitchhiking becomes an Extreme Sport

I actually find our lifestyle an adventure and other than the occasional horse-ride or skiing excursion, Thomas and I are pretty staid. Getting to waterfalls and different national parks have given us plenty of adventure.

Once on the northern part of Dominica we ended up with a guide who dumped us in the middle of nowhere because he changed the cost of the day half-way through. We had agreed that we would try to get ourselves to and from a particular waterfall but when we asked one of the locals for directions, he offered us a price that was too good to refuse. I wish we had refused.

Firstly, he had an argument with the bus driver and we ended up having to hitchhike the rest of the way. We were lucky to get a ride straight away. Then he took us on a muddy track where he showed us a view of the bay. Very nice but I had seen that view the day before when I'd gone horse-riding. He'd sat himself down on a log and I asked if he could take us to the waterfall. He looked at me bewildered and said that it was too dangerous to go there and that this view was what everyone was paying for. Not me. Thomas offered to just pay him and we would be on our way. Then he asked for more money than what we'd agreed on—he had doubled it. After a bit of haggling, we came to an agreement. I was angry with him and Thomas was concerned about how volatile he might be, so he took me aside and told me that he just wanted to get rid of him. We paid him and he sent us in the wrong direction for the waterfall. Luckily, we found a local farmer and he set us straight.

We ended up having the day that we planned—alone and walking to the waterfall for a picnic lunch. Getting a lift back down the hill wasn't so easy though. All the trucks that passed us were filled to the brim with oranges and produce for the market. After walking about five kilometres, we were picked up by some kindly gentlemen from the U.S.A. who were visiting their family on the island. We decided from that moment that we would be super cautious about hiring guides in the future.

On the advice of a young couple we'd booked into a Bed and Breakfast in a valley full of waterfalls about five hours north of Bogota. The owners briefly got us settled in and then told us that they were going off for the few days that we would be there. We were left with their delightful but non-English speaking staff. Thomas was having great difficulty understanding their Spanish as well because of their accents. My Spanish was still too basic so I was relying on gestures and the occasional word. Even getting the bus timetable into town was a challenge. Regardless of this, we decided to head off to the colonial village that was about fifteen kilometres away along a dusty road. It took us about half an hour to reach the main road where we could catch a bus. An old farmer began to walk with us and we asked him about the timetable of the bus.

Apparently, we had just missed the first bus and the next one wasn't due until midday—3 hours away. Thomas looked disgruntled but I suggested we keep going and try to hitchhike. The first vehicle that drove past us was a truck and it didn't stop but the driver waved. The second vehicle was a huge truck with a long trailer. They pulled up and the passenger motioned towards the back of the truck. I gestured towards the rear of the trailer and he shook his head and pointed just at the back of the cabin. We climbed up onto the diesel tanks on some metal grids. As we winded and twisted along the dirt road, I hung on for dear life looking at Thomas every now and then shaking my head in disbelief of our actual situation. We were grateful for the lift and thanked them upon our arrival into town. We both had sore arms for two days from hanging on so tightly. I don't recommend this at all.

Many of the islands that we have visited just didn't have a reliable transport system and we needed to thumb for a ride. I would normally not do it without Thomas or someone else but on the French islands in the Pacific, I found everyone so friendly. Even if you didn't want a lift, they would stop and offer you a lift. It became our main means of transport on most islands.

Island people are friendly and are usually happy to meet new people but I only recommend this mode of transport when travelling in pairs or in an area where you feel comfortable. There are some countries where it is actually illegal because of the crimes that have been committed along the way. So use your common sense and caution.

Panama Canal Transit

Preparation for transiting the Canal included Thomas and I being line handlers for another boat to experience what we had to do and what to expect. Anyone can put their names down on the website, which I will make a note of in the appendix, to join a boat going through the Canal. We were lucky enough to get a captain on a yacht similar in size to ours who had been through three times already. It was fascinating watching the procedures with all the different boats that pass through. The scenery was interesting as you pass through jungle and a large lake.

Confident that we had a good impression of what was to be expected, we lined up a week later for our turn. We had an adviser come on board who was to advise Thomas on what to do throughout the process. Going from the Atlantic to the Pacific takes you through a number of locks at each end of the journey. It wasn't until the last lock when disaster struck.

There was an extremely strong current and we had a strong wind pushing us forward. The yacht before us had slowed right down and Thomas had to reverse hard to avoid a collision. At that moment the coupling on the engine broke and we lost our reverse power. We were at the mercy of the current which drove us hard into a tourist boat and then into the side of the lock. Our linehandlers gallantly tried to fend us off and probably saved us from sustaining more damage than we did. Thankfully, we avoided the yacht which had young children on board. There was a crazy amount of noise and I thought we were going to be ripped apart, but in the end the damage was quite minimal. We had to wait for about a month on the Pacific side to make the repairs to the engine. The damage to the hull had to wait to be repaired because there wasn't a suitable place to dock the boat. The scratches were more aesthetic than structural and so we sailed across the Pacific as we were.

Anchoring in Beautiful Bays

People ask us what we love most about the cruising lifestyle. We would have to say that it is the beautiful bays that we get to anchor in. Thomas and I jump in unison off the side of boat when we reach a new bay. We snorkel and then either kayak or dinghy ashore to explore the terrain. We don't have to be there alone. Other cruisers are interesting and add another dimension to the adventure. However, we don't like crowds.

Night Watches and Long Passages

One of the main reasons why we got crew to cross the Atlantic was because of the different watches. It worked out well because our batteries weren't good enough to run the autopilot and we basically had to steer the whole way. But we decided that we preferred to travel alone and did several smaller crossings, like from Curacao to Colombia, which took three days, and then Colombia to Jamaica which took five days. We managed really well and decided that we would be okay for the Pacific.

We would share the day time shifts and rest whenever one or the other needed to. We would watch a movie in the evening and then begin our shifts afterwards. I would do the first three hour shift, keeping an eye on the weather, the sails and looking out for other boats. We didn't see anyone. We also have an automatic transponder that would inform us of any commercial vessels in range. Thomas would then do the next three hours then, he would wake me for a two hour shift and then he would have the one leading into daylight hours. He would then let me sleep in.

Both our longer passages took twenty-one days. That's twenty-one days seeing no one but each other and coping with life at sea. I would take my headphones each day and dance on the deck, hanging on to parts of the boat. Thomas would mainly read. Meal times were special because they punctuated the day. Sometimes, we would eat out of bowls because it was just too rough. I once served

Thomas spaghetti on a plate and it all landed on the table beside his plate when we rocked. I learned never to serve spaghetti on a passage. There's not a lot to do on a passage except relax and take it easy. I quite like them but Thomas worries about the boat and gets a bit bored. It always means arriving in a new exciting country and it's so wonderful when you arrive.

Bangs Squeaks and Rattles

The amount of noise the boat makes on a crossing can unnerve the calmest of captains. When we were crossing the Pacific we were having some problems with the rudder and then a terribly high pitched squeak began. Thomas thought it was the autopilot and exclaimed that was all we needed. I went up into the cockpit and turned off the autopilot and steered. The squeak persisted. I heard a spray of water and looked just beside the boat. There was a pod of cheeky pilot whales chatting away. The captain was very relieved.

Please send me your travel anecdotes for others to enjoy by sending them to gaylyn@practical-spiritual-guide.com

Not only will others enjoy them but you'll be able to offer up-to-date information on some locations.

Mystery, Mayhem and Spirits

It was actually my ex-husband's idea to build a home out of old railway carriages. He'd seen it done down in South Australia and thought they would make a unique home. I agreed. The plan was to put them on our hectare/3 ½ acre property in the bush at Balgal Beach, just north of Townsville. We listed our name with the railway department and waited until some were available. We were hoping for four but the two we were allocated ended up being substantial enough to turn into a home in the beginning. It was 1990 and they cost $500 each and cost us $3,500 to transport them and place them on steel stumps on the property. It was a bargain. Putting on the power, septic tank and water doubled that cost but it was still a reasonable investment.

I remembered that when I went to inspect them, the railway guy smiled at me and told me they were special. Particularly the one we were standing in. I looked around and thought that it wasn't as impressive as the one he'd shown me previously but I just shook it off. That one was identified as DAV 997. The other had wrought iron at the end of small verandas and pressed iron ceilings throughout. 997 had ordinary wire criss-crossed on the veranda and plain painted Masonite ceilings. I couldn't work out what he was talking about but he knew the carriages' secret, I'm sure. It took us a while to scrub and make them comfortable to inhabit but the work was worth it. They were certainly different and full of character.

We turned 997 into the bedrooms and the other carriage, 998, was converted into the lounge, dining room and kitchen. We'd placed them into an 'L' shape 120 metres from the road so they were in amongst the trees. It didn't take us very long before the spirits in 997 began to become restless. I was getting messages of violence and fear. I couldn't work out what had happened. They were guard vans, where the guard would rest and luggage was stored. I was trying to gather more information from them but at the same time, I didn't want my home to be haunted. I wanted a place of rest.

I knew they were there but I'd just started to teach so I didn't really have much time to focus on this issue. They would come and ask me to 'find out' and I would ignore them. There were times when the dog would stop and be looking in mid-air at something and let out little barks like he did when he was trying to talk to us about something. It was as if they were communicating with him. Life went on and they must have tired of me asking them to go away as I was too busy.

One night I was in a half-sleep state when they actually lifted the top half of my body up from the bed. I wasn't floating, as my bottom was still on the bed. As I opened my eyes in amazement, I was confronted with a hideous distorted face screaming at me just centimetres from my face. Then, whatever it was, dropped me hard back to the bed. It was enough to wind me. Shaking, I turned to see my sleeping husband undisturbed. I just lay there trying to work out if what had just happened was real or not. I decided that I better stop ignoring them and told them so. I announced that I would listen to whatever they wanted to tell me. I'd never had an actual physical encounter with spirit before like that and I have to admit that it gave me a scare. It was months before I had any more messages in relation to the carriage. Maybe they thought they were a bit rough on me. I was doing some renovations and decided that I needed to visit the railway workshops down in Ipswich to find some more light fittings. I was getting messages of confirmation.

As I arrived at the workshops I was greeted by two elderly gentlemen who were keen to take me through the labyrinth of buildings and passages to get to where one of them remembered seeing some old fittings. They were chatty folk and I could hardly get a word in. They began chatting in an animated way about the old carriages and telling me that some of them had a colourful history. So much so that some of the carriages even appeared to have a personality. The carriages were first built in 1921 and had seen a lot of events. As the dialogue between the two men continued they began to personify their descriptions. They spoke of the old carriage that used to transport the lepers down to the wharf to catch the ferry to the quarantine island, they spoke of carrying the troops around Australia during World War II as if they were reliving the events themselves. Then one of them said, "And don't forget about that one that the murders happened in." The hair went up on the back of my neck and I knew it was my carriage. The railway men continued their banter, filling in some details including that two men were murdered in a sleeper van back in the late thirties just north of Brisbane. One of them finally announced, "Yep, that one was 997." I must have turned pale because they stopped and turned to me and asked, "Are you all right Love?" I replied by telling them that my vans were guard vans and couldn't possibly be the one involved in the murder they described. "Oh, but they all got changed over to guard vans in the fifties." I disclosed that I owned 997 and 998. "Wow, you're lucky!" they responded.

I didn't mention my encounter with spirit to the men. They didn't seem the open types but they were very helpful. They told me that they thought it was a botched robbery and a guard had interrupted him. They told me that he didn't get away with much money but he got caught a few days later disguised as a maid in a hotel in Sydney anyway. It was his three day growth that had given him away. It was quite an ordeal for Australia in those times to have a murderer. His name was Kopot and the letters from his name were turned into the acronym 'Killer Of People On Trains'. They thought that the culprit had died of a brain tumour in jail 6 months later before he went to trial. Still in a state of shock about my carriage, I went away with unanswered questions.

Later during that visit to the south of Queensland I toddled off to the state library to seek out more information only to discover that I needed an actual date of the incident to be able to do any research on the microfiche. I visited a railway museum and they knew nothing about the event. I went home to the carriages after my holiday was over and upon the next encounter with the spirits I told them that it was all okay because he didn't get much money and he died soon after. Whoever was there just up and left immediately. I tried to call them back as I wanted more details but I never felt them again. It was another five years before I would gain more insight.

I had moved to the south-east corner of the state to Toowoomba and I was mentioning my ghosts to a colleague when she was telling me about spiritual visitors in an old house she was renovating. She delighted in telling me that she knew the story as her dad had worked in the railways and she'd found a newspaper clipping about the murders when she was pulling up some floor covering from her old house and had sent it to him. The best part was that she still had a copy. The clipping she sent me was about Kopot's arrest. There was a picture of a very unattractive woman and I thought that it was no wonder that he got caught because he made an ugly woman, but then

I read the caption under the picture and it was a picture of the station mistress from the station where he had boarded making a statement about him. Oops! So I never actually got to see a picture of him but I went back to the state library and looked up the newspapers from the date of the murders. It was front page news and there in print was the identification of the carriage where the murders took place—997 and a photo revealed the plain criss-cross wire on the end of the veranda. There was no doubt that it was my carriage.

A Brief Philosophy about Nature Cure

Nature Cure had its foundations established in the 19th century when the medical system was beginning to be recognised as the main authority on health. The priest and shamans had shared almost an equal standing on the matter until then. It challenges the mainstream paradigm that a chemical concoction will remedy the ills of the body. Basically Nature Cure claims that is the body that heals itself, not an outside influence in the form of a drug. An individual organism requires the correct environmental conditions to enable it to repair, rejuvenate and reproduce damaged cells. My time studying Nature Cure involved learning about these conditions, practising methods of diagnosis, studying the constitution of individual clientele and advising them on a program that would lead them to a state of wellness.

What I really love about the approach was that there is nothing to sell. Just good advice and that advice comes from the universal laws of nature. Once you know them, you see them in everything around you. It is a truth that is refreshing. It allows an individual to be in charge of his or her own health and know how to respond when things go wrong. Herbs and remedies fall into the same category as medicine with this philosophy. If it isn't a nourishing food then it doesn't go into the body. It is an inexpensive approach and a great alternative when you look around and see all the money—demanding methods drilled into us through advertising. Most of these advertisements claim that you will have great health—if only you're prepared to pay the price. It fits nicely with my views on consumerism and the assault that we all have to contend with through advertising. My knowledge provides me with a freedom to travel anywhere in the world and to know that I am safe because I know how to look after myself.

I know that by following this philosophy I have had a healthier and more active life so far. I have my mentors and teachers, Katie and Kevin Hinton to thank for advising me and I recommend you visit their website at www.hintonhealth.com.au to explore the concepts further or contact me on my website if you would like to meet up for a consultation.

The Condensed Version of Thomas' and my Love Story

Satisfied that I'd reached most of my travelling goals about being independent, travelling on a budget, meeting amazing people and trusting the Universe, it was time to really take my hands off the steering wheel and let the forces of the cosmos lead me to the next phase of my existence. I was cruising on an Italian yacht in the northern sector of the Greek Isles when I made up my mind that it was just too hot to do my planned land tour of Turkey. A friend had asked me to meet up in Malta but I was determined to stick with a major component of my journey to visit Turkey. We briefly discussed options of her meeting me there but she could see complications in the plan.

As an alternative to a land tour in the heat I began to seek out a Turkish yacht on the Find a Crew website. I wasn't receiving any responses from Turkish captains and I began to look for alternatives in Croatia and other areas that I hadn't considered. A new chat feature had just been activated for premium members and a quick glance at who was on line revealed only one captain in the Mediterranean.

It was Thomas. So I struck up a conversation with him and he suggested we have a Skype call. We did and I warmed to him immediately. He was open and funny and we had a good time. He explained that he hadn't been sailing for long and he needed some crew to get to Malta where he was picking up some new sails. Bells were ringing at the coincidence of the situation. I weighed my options. I could fly to Mallorca where he was based, sail to Malta with him and then visit my friend. He told me he had crew meeting him in Malta so I knew I would be able to stay in Malta if I chose to or return to Spain with him. Then I could visit Spain, a country I'd never been to before. Once it cooled down a bit, I could return to Turkey and travel in the cooler weather. I looked into the cost of flights and they were reasonable. I was getting positive vibes about the captain and the journey so I contacted him to let him know that I would crew for him.

Thomas met me at the bus stop and the first thing I thought was, 'Oh, wow. He's better looking than what he looked on Skype.' As I was there as crew though, I had no expectations. I was happy to have my own cabin as I'd had to sleep in the saloon of the Italian boat. After a bit of shopping we returned to the boat. It was more beautiful than I expected. I unpacked the few items I would need and settled in. It was quite warm and we swam in the bay where Qi, (pronounced Chi), was anchored. We stayed up nearly all night talking and laughing. He made sure I was relaxed and comfortable.

After a day of sightseeing, we prepared for the journey. He had taken me to all the types of sights that I loved and then we went to a funky cafe where plenty of vegetarian tapas were on offer. He was thoughtful and kind. I took over the shopping role immediately as I'd planned on cooking. We quickly fell into a routine of swimming, chatting and staying up late sharing stories. Thomas had only recently become single after a long relationship had ended but he had done a lot of travelling with his ex. She was a travel journalist and he had amazing stories of their adventures. I was loving the conversation and his company.

It didn't take very long before we both realised that we were attracted to each other. One day when I was steering across to the island of Menorca, he made the statement, "I wish my friends could see me now. Sitting back here sailing in the Balearic Islands on my own yacht with a beautiful woman at the helm." Ah, I thought. He thinks I'm beautiful. That evening under a full moon I talked him into going for a late night swim. The sultry air, the clear night and the cool water created the backdrop for romance. We teased and frolicked in the water and the playfulness continued back on the boat.

Our romance continued to blossom and it was everything I'd ever hoped for. We sailed, explored islands and swam the days away. He was setting the table each night with a candle flitting away in the breeze, (I later found out that was because of the lack of having a suitable light—not because it was romantic, but it made an impression on me). I was cooking delicious meals and every night was a wonderful adventure as we got to know each other better.

We coped with an emergency when the propeller fell off on the first major crossing we did to Sardinia, and we worked well as a team on the boat in general. While we waited for a new propeller to arrive we explored the island by hiking and soon discovered that we liked to visit the same sorts of places. Once everything was back in order with the propeller we moved onto Sicily. We were being treated to displays of comets each night and after a special lasagne dinner he invited me to the front deck to lie on the cushions under the stars. He asked me if I would keep sailing with him and never leave his boat. I was dumbstruck because as I was making the lasagne I was thinking that it tasted so good that he would want to marry me after eating it. So, I was thinking to myself, 'did I put a spell on the lasagne or does he really mean this?' I didn't answer him straight away. My mind was racing.

I hardly slept as I was so excited about his offer. It wasn't a marriage proposal but it was something better. I was trying to work out if this was what the Universe had prepared me for. I would have to sell my property and my car so that I could afford to keep travelling and I would have to apply for another years' leave from work. Not seeing my son, his baby son and my daughter for long intervals while we'd be sailing would be hard I knew. It was a huge decision but I was really just working out how I could do it. I'd already began to wonder how I was ever going to move on away from him. I knew straight away that I wanted to say yes. That evening he took me

190   Backpacker's Practical and Spiritual Guide to the Universe

out to dinner. As we dined in a small restaurant overlooking the sea from a cliff, I shared my thoughts with him. He responded with, "Is that a yes?" and he kissed me passionately. An old man was wandering through the crowd selling roses from his garden and Thomas bought all of them from him. I knew I'd made the right choice. This man would always make me feel special.

By the time we made it to Malta we were a couple. My friend's husband had also arrived in Malta and he was a friend of mine too. We dined together and they adored my new Captain. We toured around the islands that make up the country of Malta, exploring caves and exquisite bays. Sailing into the historical fortified city of Valletta is still a highlight of my sailing experiences. It was the month of August when the Maltese celebrate saint's birthdays and we had fireworks every night and church bells ringing. It was a magical experience.

Our adventures continue and they probably make for a whole other book. We are taking time out at the moment living on the boat in the city of Brisbane. I've returned to teaching for a year and a bit to help fill my cruising kitty again. My independence is still important to me and I always like to pay my own way. I strongly believe that there is no such thing as a free lunch. Especially in a relationship.

Notes

Appendix

Recipes

First Shop Menu

Stir fry, curry and rice, crepes and curry, fried rice, frittata, scrambled eggs

➤ Stir fry—time: 25 minutes if you're a fast chopper

Ingredients
Any vegetables available
2 eggs, soya sauce
A teaspoon of sugar or honey
1 stock cube
Thin spaghetti or rice noodles.
Cooking oil
Extras like tofu or small cuts of meat, chicken or fish marinated in soya sauce, water, or honey

Equipment
Fry pan or wok
Large plate
Spatula, (egg flip) or wooden spoon
Sharp knife
Chopping board
Saucepan
Strainer

Method

1. Boil your noodles or spaghetti. If you're using thin spaghetti then add a bit of soya sauce.

2. Cut most of the vegetables into 'Juliet' (long thin slices), slice cauliflower or broccoli thinly too. Make eight wedges like cutting an orange for the onion.

3. Mix the two eggs in a bowl and fry in a pan or a wok on a low heat like an omelette. Turn over once. Remove and place on a plate.

4. Cook any meats or tofu next making the element slightly hotter. Remove and place on a plate.

5. Fry any onion with ginger and mushrooms until the onions are clear and place on the plate.

6. Add any extra spices such as cumin or coriander with the onion mix.

7. Add the vegetables that take longer to cook such as carrot and cauliflower and stir around for 1 minute.

8. Lower the heat a fraction and place a lid on the wok so the vegetables can cook through a bit for two minutes.

9. Stir every minute and replace the lid until the cauliflower is almost soft.

10. Slice the egg, add everything together including the extras, fast cooking vegetables such as cabbage or broccoli and noodles.

11. Add ¼ cup of soya sauce, a spoonful of honey or sugar and one crushed stock cube. Stir sauce through the mixture and replace the lid for two minutes.

12. The fast cooking vegetables should be just about cooked. Remove from heat before they are fully cooked as they keep cooking for a short time. This makes a crunchy healthy stir fry.

➤ Curry and Rice—30 min cook and preparation time

Ingredients
Any local vegetables that you like cut in cubes
Onions diced in large pieces
Ginger cut in extra small squares
Curry powder or paste
Stock cube
Can of coconut milk
Rice
Cooking oil

Equipment
2 medium saucepans with at least one lid
Chopping board
Sharp knife
Wooden spoon or spatula

Method
1. Place one saucepan on a low-medium heat and place a spoonful of oil into it.
2. Place two cups of rice in and stir around coating all the rice with oil.
3. Add two cups of water and turn up the heat to bring it to the boil.
4. Stir a few times.
5. Once boiling, place a lid on it and turn to the lowest heat for 10 minutes.
6. Then remove it from the heat altogether and leave the lid on so it continues to cook. (This makes enough rice to use leftovers for fried rice the next day.)
7. While the rice is cooking place the slow cooking vegetables in the second saucepan with a teaspoonful of oil, (such as yam, sweet potato, potato and carrot.) Stir occasionally and let cook for 5 minutes.

8. Add curry paste or powder, stockcube, onion and other fast cooking vegetables, (such as cauliflower and pumpkin). Stir for 2 minutes.
9. Add the coconut milk. Stir and let cook at a low simmer for 10 minutes.
10.Serve with the rice.

➤ **Crepes and Curry**—15 minutes preparation time

Ingredients
Left over curry
1 egg
1 cup of milk
¾ cup of flour
Butter or oil

Equipment
Small frypan
Spatula, (egg flip)
Small saucepan
Small bowl
Plate
Fork
Dessert spoon

Method

1. If your curry is a bit dry, add a small amount of water to it before reheating. Heat up on a low element. Stir and check occasionally while you cook the crepes.
2. Crepes—Beat your egg into a bowl
3. Add the milk, mixing as you go.
4. Slowly add the flour until you have a consistency of a creamy liquid soap
5. Mix with your fork a bit more until the batter is smooth.
6. Heat up the small frypan on a medium—hot element.
7. Add a teaspoon of butter or oil to the pan and four spoonfuls

of mixture.

8. Quickly pick the pan up by the handle, (goes without saying but you just never know eh?), and swirl the mixture around to make a circle.
9. Cook for 2 minutes and then flip.
10. Cook for another minute and then place on a plate.
11. Repeat process.

Will make about 10 so invite a guest or have some Nutella ready for the left overs. They will keep and reheat easily too. Serve with curry and maybe a small salad at the side.

➢ **Fried Rice**—15 minutes preparation and cooking time

Ingredients
Left over rice
Onions
Any other vegetables cut up finely
Cooking oil
2 eggs
Soy sauce
Stock cube
(Add a teaspoon of honey to make the sauce thicker if you like)

Equipment
Medium sized fry pan
Chopping board
Sharp knife
Small bowl
Fork

Method

1. Mix eggs in a small bowl and fry on a medium heat like an omelette. Flip when the bottom is cooked. Remove from heat and slice into strips.
2. Chop all ingredients quite small
3. Fry vegetables on a medium heat in 2 teaspoons of cooking oil for 3 minutes
4. Add a bit more oil and add the rice stirring it through the oil for 2 minutes.
5. Add 1/4 of a cup of soya sauce and the stock cube.
6. Stir for another 2 minutes and serve.

➤ Frittata—preparation and cooking time 35 minutes

Ingredients
Potatoes
Pumpkin or sweet potato
Onion
Capsicum
Any other vegetables diced small
Small amount of grated cheese if available
Cooking oil
4 eggs
½ cup of milk
Stock cube crumbled

Equipment
Fry pan with lid
Chopping board
Sharp knife
Small bowl

Method

1. Peel and slice potato, pumpkin and sweet potato very thinly.
2. Dice the remainder of the vegetables.
3. Mix eggs and milk in a small bowl and add grated cheese.
4. Fry up potato, pumpkin and sweet potato but keep them firm still.
5. Turn the heat down quite low and place the sliced vegetables around the bottom of the pan.
6. Pour in the bowl of egg and cheese and place the lid on.
7. Cook for 10 minutes before checking.
8. Make sure the bottom isn't burning. If it is, place the fry pan upside down onto the lid and flip the whole frittata over.
9. Cook for another 10 minutes. If you get the heat low enough to begin with, you shouldn't need to do that.
10. Serve with a small salad or wrap for a picnic lunch.

➤ Scrambled Eggs—5 minutes preparation and cooking time

Ingredients
3 eggs
¼ cup of milk

Equipment
Fry pan
Spatula, (egg flip)
Fork

Method
1. Break eggs into a fry pan and mix in with a fork and add milk.
2. Place fry pan over a low heat and continuously stir the eggs around with the spatula until they are fluffy and cooked.
3. Add cheese if you like.

Second Shop Menu

Tortillas, tuna/mushroom pasta, Stove top pizza, wraps

➤ Tortillas—10 minutes preparation and cooking

Ingredients
Tortillas
Red kidney beans
Taco mix or chilli
Tomato sauce
Stock cube
Salad
Onion
Cooking oil

Equipment
Sauce pan
Wooden spoon
A plate
Chopping board
Sharp knife
Can opener

Method

1. Cut up salad and dice onions/chilli.
2. Put a teaspoonful of oil in the saucepan at a low-medium heat.
3. Fry onions and chilli or taco mix for two minutes.
4. Add drained kidney beans and add ¼ cup of tomato sauce and stock cube.
5. Cook for 5 more minutes stirring occasionally.
6. Heat up tortillas by placing them on top of the saucepan with the beans or use a small fry pan with a small amount of oil.
7. Serve with salad.

➢ Tuna/Mushroom Pasta—
Preparation and cooking 20 minutes

Ingredients
Tuna or mushrooms
Can of diced tomatoes or a 250 mL cartoon or can of cream/soy or rice alternative
Tomato sauce if using can of tomatoes
Stock cube
Onion
Cooking oil
Pasta of choice
Salad

Equipment
Chopping board
Sharp knife
2 saucepans

Method
1. Follow the directions for pasta and put this on first.
2. Dice onion and cook in a teaspoonful of oil for 2 minutes on a low-medium heat.
3. Add stock cube, mushrooms or tuna and cook for another 2 minutes.
4. Add the cream or tomatoes and tomato sauce and let simmer on a low heat for 7 minutes.
5. Serve over pasta with a side salad.

➤ Stove top Pizza—
preparation and cooking time 30 minutes

Ingredients
Flat bread
Cooking oil
Grated cheese
Onion
Capsicum
Toppings of choice
Tomato sauce
Any Italian herbs that you find on the free shelf
Salad
Optional toppings: thinly sliced pumpkin, potato or sweet potato with
a bit of pesto or shredded spinach and feta cheese

Equipment
Spatula, (egg flip)
Fry pan with a lid
Chopping board
Sharp knife

Method
1. Chop all the toppings and grate the cheese first.
2. If using sliced pumpkin etc slightly fry these in oil before placing on pizza.
3. Fry one side of the flat bread in a teaspoonful of oil on a low heat until it is lightly brown.
4. Turn the heat down as low as it will go.
5. Flip the flat bread once and spread tomato sauce over it then place some of the toppings evenly over the browned side.
6. Sprinkle the cheese on.
7. Place a lid on and relax while it cooks or make your salad.

8. Use other fry pans if they are available to make the amount you want.
9. Check the bottom of the pizza every couple of minutes. Remove from heat briefly if it is burning.
10. Serve with salad.

➢ Wraps—preparation and cooking time 20 minutes

Ingredients
1 boiled egg per wrap
Lettuce
Tomato
Cucumber
Peanut butter
Wraps, (flatbread, roti or tortillas)

Equipment
Small saucepan
Spoon
Chopping board
Sharp knife
Fry pan if heating up wraps

Method—Boil eggs for 8 minutes
1. Heat up wraps by putting the number you want on a low heat in a fry pan with the lid on.
2. Turn every minute.
3. Remove from heat.
4. Spread peanut butter onto wrap.
5. Slice the cooked egg and put on it.
6. Add salad.
7. Add any other sauces you may desire. Sweet chilli sauce goes great with this.

Notes

Helpful Websites and Contacts

The websites that I refer to during my actual travel are usually very topic related. I will direct my searches for a particular attraction or to meet my immediate needs. These websites are too varied to list here. What I have included are the sites that lead to planning major parts of a journey.

http://www.practical-spiritual-guide.com/ This is my website where you will find more budgeting tips, recipes, a story sharing place, information about tarot card readings and naturopathy consultations.

Contact gaylyn@practical-spiritual-guide.com

Information on Nature Cure naturopathy on www.hintonhealth.com.au

For travel options

www.helpx.net—for work exchange. Working in exchange for lodgings

www.workaway.info—for volunteer work with private families and businesses in exchange for lodgings

www.wwoofinternational.org—for volunteer work on organic farms around the world

www.couchsurfing.com.—for free accommodation, cultural exchange and local experiences

www.gumtree.com.au—for ride share and accommodation options

www.craigslist.org—for ride share and accommodation options

http://thesavvybackpacker.com/backpack-europe-planning/—for planning to travel to Europe in particular

www.hostelbookers.com—for booking inexpensive accommodation

www.hostelworld.com—for booking inexpensive accommodation

http://chickenfeettravels.com —for adventure tours in South-east Asia

www.panhandlers.com—for having the opportunity to join a boat to transit the Panama Canal—set two days aside for this. You get a feed and a return bus fare for helping out a skipper on a yacht but be prepared for a bit of a workout at each lock.

References

The official website of *The Secret*

http://thesecret.tv

Sproats, Joseph (2011) Creating Wealth Platypus Wealth Publishers, Townsville

Tan, Chade-Meng (2012) Search Inside Yourself Harper One Publishers, New York

ISBN 978-0-06-211692-5

Wilde, Stuart (1998) The Little Money Bible Hay House Publishers, Carlsbad, CA

ISBN 0-947266-38-0

Nicolai C. Stigar

Norwegian Animator/Comicbook-artist/Illustrator

Printed in Australia
AUOC02n0814040417
284472AU00002B/2/P

9 781943 265718